INTRODUCTION
TO SOCIAL DREAMING

INTRODUCTION TO SOCIAL DREAMING
Transforming Thinking

W. Gordon Lawrence

KARNAC
LONDON   NEW YORK

Figure 3, p. 33, reprinted with the permission of SUNY (the State University of New York) from E. Hartmann, "The Psychology and Physiology of Dreaming: A New Synthesis." In: L. Gamwell (Ed.), *Dreams 1900–2000: Science, Art, and the Unconscious Mind* (Fig. 2.4, p. 67). New York: Cornell University Press, 2000.

Figure 4, p. 84, reprinted with the permission of Simon & Schuster Adult Publishing Group from *The Dreaming Universe* (Fig. 7, p. 163) by Fred Alan Wolf, Ph.D. Copyright © 1994 by Wolf Productions.

First published in 2005 by
H. Karnac (Books) Ltd.
6 Pembroke Buildings, London NW10 6RE

British Library Cataloguing in Publication Data

A C.I.P. for this book is available from the British Library

ISBN: 1-85575-342-1

10 9 8 7 6 5 4 3 2 1

Edited, designed, and produced by Communication Crafts

Printed in Great Britain

www.karnacbooks.com

CONTENTS

ACKNOWLEDGEMENTS

I am grateful to Dr Kenneth Eisold of New York, who read versions of the drafts and added to the text, also to Drs Zeborah Schachtel, Victoria Hamilton, and Judit Szekacs. To John Clare and Ali Zarbafi, who cooperated on the Case Study in chapter ten, I owe my thanks. To Bipin Patel I am indebted for his support of the social dreaming project from the beginning. Any mistakes of thinking, fact, and any omissions are mine. Also I owe my gratitude to the thousands of people who have participated in social dreaming matrices in different countries. Because they have extended my thinking, I now respect and value them as colleagues.

W. Gordon Lawrence

Preface

When social dreaming was discovered at the Tavistock Institute in 1982, the term "social dreaming" did not exist in any of the literature as far as the writer was able to check. The task of this short book is to explain social dreaming by situating it in the context of thinking, culture, and knowledge and to distinguish how it differs from conventional, therapeutic dreaming, making the case for how it can be used in systems, like business organizations, educational institutions, the churches, hospitals, and with any professional groups of people, such as firemen or students.

For the moment, until an opportunity is made to explain it and its terms further in the text that follows, it can be said that social dreaming is an opportunity to share one's dreams with others in a matrix. The focus is on the dream, not the dreamer. The dreamer recounts his/her dream to the others in the matrix, but the dream is not a personal possession, for it captures the social, political, institutional, and spiritual aspects of the dreamer's social environment. The meaning of the dream unfolds through the use of free association and amplification to give form to the echoes of thinking and thought that exist in the space between the minds of individuals living in the social environment.

INTRODUCTION
TO SOCIAL DREAMING

The history of social dreaming

As the discoverer of the social dreaming matrix, I took the first steps on the journey of dreaming socially in 1982 at the Tavistock Institute. Since then, others have joined me. From the early 1980s, social dreaming matrices have been conducted in Israel, Sweden, Finland, Holland, Denmark, Germany, France, Italy, the United Kingdom, Ireland, India, Australia, the United States of America, and Rwanda.

From all these matrices, it has been learned that social dreaming does illumine life in institutions and enterprises, such as commercial companies, as it makes manifest the infinite knowing that is present in these systems.

What were the steps of this journey of discovery?

As human beings, we learn from experience. In normal conversation, someone will offer a dream: "I had a dream last night." We then enter the surreal world of the night of the narrator. The temptation is to "interpret" the dream in terms of the individual, because that gives us power in the relationship. Also, it is the way we have learned to deal with the gift of dreaming. What happens when we give up the necessity to express dominance? We enter the dream, on its terms, when we listen to the experience of the dream as it is recounted. Interpretation is the death of new knowledge, for it is always grounded in old understandings. Only working hypotheses can help us to arrive at the truth of what might be reality and the significance of the meaning of dreams.

Similarly, anthropological studies of dreaming focus on the relationship between dreaming and culture, not on aspects of the individual dreamer.

The social dreaming journey started from working in groups when I was joint director of the Tavistock Institute's Group Relations Programme. Dreams were presented in the course of a group's life. It was difficult to work with them, because the idea of analysis of the individual dreamer was taboo. This would have been contrary to the task of enabling people to find their authority from the context of the group (Lawrence, 2000b). It was clear, however, that these dreams always illustrated what was taking place in the life of the group.

These experiences were not sufficient to formulate the idea of social dreaming. The missing component came from a reading of Charlotte Beradt's *The Third Reich of Dreams* (1968). Beradt was a journalist who lived and worked in Hitler's Germany. She invited medical practitioner friends to record the dreams of patients as part of their medical examination. The Fascist regime controlled the thinking of the German population.

The dreaming and dreams derived from what she called "man's paradoxical existence under a twentieth-century totalitarian regime" (Beradt, 1968, p. 15). The dreams she recorded were not produced by conflicts of the inner, private realm, but were the result of the political realities of the public domain and the ensuing disturbed human relations. She writes, "there is no façade to conceal associations, and no outside person need provide the link between dream image and reality—this the dreamer himself does" (p. 15).

This was the clinching evidence that led to the journey into the world of social dreaming, which is the twentieth-century method of engaging with the continual human struggle between the primordial elements of being human and the creative imagination.

Over the years, the development of social dreaming has given rise to a number of dreams on the part of the writer. The most telling was the Blind Architect Dream (Lawrence, 1991).

> The dream was of being *at a dinner party in the Paris apartment of friends. During it, a visitor arrived from the provinces. He had to get to a new cathedral because he was involved in its construction, and I seemed to be the only person who knew where it was. He was very insistent that he should go by taxi, as he had travelled a long distance by train that day. I went down with him to the street where the taxi was waiting and gave precise instructions to the driver. It was only later in the dream when talking with the fellow guests that I realized that the stranger was a blind architect. I remember thinking in the dream, "Who would employ a blind architect?" A deaf composer is possible. Beethoven proved that. But a blind architect?*

What comes to mind is that in order to see, human beings have to make themselves temporarily blind. To be sure, social dreaming is a way of seeing dreaming with new eyes and developing an understanding of a dimension of life that has been lost sight of as our civilization has become ever more triumphant.

When it was discovered in the early 1980s, the notion that dreaming could be examined with a set of people was quite radical. The received truth was that dreams and dreaming could only be conducted by a psychoanalyst and an analysand. Any other configuration was understood to be erroneous. Nevertheless, the writer persevered to discover with colleagues what has become the content of this monograph.

CHAPTER ONE

Social dreaming in a company

E arly on it was thought that social dreaming could have applications for business people. An opportunity came with a French group of companies. Each year for five years the president of the group convened a seminar for his senior managers. The writer had been an organizational consultant working with the president for about eight years. The purpose of the seminar was to reflect on the state of the company by identifying the pressing problems and issues the group was facing in a changing commercial environment. From this analysis the seminar considered what the group could become to realize its goals. Each seminar lasted for four days, and they were convened in various countries, such as Spain, France, and Bulgaria. At the fifth seminar it was decided to hold a social dreaming matrix (SDM) each morning for an hour, as the first event of the day. The language was French, with occasional forays into English.

The hypothesis that managers with pressing business problems could benefit from the experience of social dreaming as part of the seminar was offered. Consequently, it was tried with the senior managers of the group (Lawrence, 1998b). The following very truncated summary, which has been disguised to preserve confidentiality, may serve to introduce some aspects of a social dreaming matrix and give examples of the quality of thinking it engenders. The purpose of the matrix was to share dreams and to associate to them as freely as possible.

The first matrix opened with some observations on the nature of dreaming, and some participants wondered whether they actually dream at all. They concluded that they dreamed more when they were on holiday than when they were at work.

One manager, who had a dream of being *on an escalator*, expressed doubts about the value and possible risks of dreaming. He had a feeling of being off-balance. The escalator symbolized links between waking and dreaming. At the same time, it highlighted the levels of consciousness where sometimes the dream is more real or pertinent than what is perceived in waking life, as well as the presence of unconscious thinking and no-thinking, which is always putting one off balance but is, ideally, always in an interdependent, or symbiont, relationship with consciousness.

Another manager followed by saying that normally he did not remember his dreams, but he was able to recall some elements of a dream the night before. His dream was in relation to the catalogue of his company. (For a mail-order company, the catalogue is the key selling tool, and thus its quality is critical for this company.)

> There was a fashion presentation that was taking place on the gangway of a boat. The presentation was being photographed. The feeling of the place was of elegance, with a lot of people present. It was, however, cold. The people present were fashion designers, and the atmosphere was a little mad, even bizarre. There was a lot of light from the sun and much movement among the people present.

The dreamer ended his description by saying that they were not dealing with issues of fashion in his company.

It was intriguing that one of the first dreams should be about work. Can we assume that the gangway [*passerolle*], in addition to paralleling the escalator, mentioned above as a transition to the domain of the conscious, symbolized the catalogue issued by the company, with its marketing strategies to sell its goods to potential customers either on the "boat" or the "quay"? In actuality, the company has an attractive catalogue and even has what are called "best-sellers", but it does not yet have the amount of turnover needed. This is very worrying for all the people in the company: there is stress, and a sense of persecution has grown because of their comparative lack of success. The market is a cold place in reality.

The dream was followed by what the participants called a "flash". This dreamer had one, which was, *"Faith saves one"*. The theme of faith had been running through the seminar in other events.

A later dream in the sequence follows.

> *The dreamer is walking on the left side of a road. Coming towards him is his President, who is also on the left of the road. The right-hand side of the road is piled high with stones. The dreamer is not sure whether these stones are the result of a rock-fall, or whether they are waiting to be used in the rebuilding of the road. He says that he is not sure whether they are there as a result of a natural destruction or whether they are waiting for use in construction. The road itself is well marked—but is the line marking the centre of the road or the edge of it?*

This dream echoes the actual political situation of the dreamer as a new managing director working with the president who had, up to now, also held the role of managing director. We thought that the stones on the right—one of the president's names is Pierre [*pierre* = stone]—represented the company, which has experienced a downturn in trading. Could the company be turned around—that is, is reconstruction possible—or is it in a disastrous, ruinous state? Where are the limits to any future growth of the company? The unasked questions for all the members of the seminar were: Can the new managing director work with the president? Will they have a confrontational relationship or work in harmony? Who is clinging to which of the company's values and faith?

Another dreamer is

on the gangway of a boat; he cannot see anything because there is fog, but everyone assures him that when the weather is good, it is a very nice view.

One set of associations was to the present state of the companies seeing the gangway (catalogue), again, as the commercial link between the companies and their customers. While matters may now be bad, perhaps better trading conditions will come when the fog lifts.

Another dreamer said that he had a dream but

in the dream he experienced himself as conscious and awake. He is speaking to another managing director about a new marketing manager who is being transferred from one company in the group to another. (This was true.) *The dreamer finds himself saying that this marketing manager speaks English very well—indeed, would have an A grade. The president reacts to this by saying, "You see, you don't have enough confidence in people. Leave me alone, I am going to read the Bible." He does so, and in the dream he is facing one of the takers* (hosts)[1], *who is reading the Bible (the Book of Baruch) in English.*

The president is reading the Book of Baruch, which does not appear in the King James I Version but in the Apocrypha, having been excluded from the Protestant canon at the time of the Reformation. Baruch appears in French Bibles. As far as we have been able to check, Baruch was important for giving a message to the conquered people who were under Babylonian rule. He also saved the religious furnishings of the temple after a Holocaust. The president is a Catholic, while it is well-enough known that the consultant is not. So the dream expressed something of the difficulty that the dreamer has in understanding why a French president should have an English-speaking consultant in his work role. And what is the nature of the transference, or authority, feelings between them? Who has access to what kind of knowledge? The possible reason for the selection of Baruch was that it might express something of the phenomenal role of the president in the group—that is, trying to celebrate and maintain its French identity in an international context. Embedded in this dream was the idea of persecution and disaster, but also the idea of being awake, in touch with what is really happening.

The company politics were revealed in an astounding dream:

> *There is a town in which lives a Little Vassal. The Fat Duke comes to visit, and the Little Vassal welcomes him to the town. There is in the place a big armchair, which could also be a throne, and it is used for that purpose on occasion. When the Little Vassal sits in the armchair, the whole town is illuminated, and the longer he sits in the chair, the more intense is the light. In order to have the very best light possible, it is suggested by the townspeople that the Fat Duke should also sit in the armchair with the Little Vassal.*
>
> *While the two are sitting in the chair, the son of the Little Vassal, who is an architect, is installing a mobile, which is in the form of a spiral, attaching it to the ceiling of the room in which the Little Vassal and the Fat Duke are seated. It is a very innovative and attractive mobile. The Fat Duke expresses disapproval.*
>
> *The Little Vassal finds that there are two ways to sit on the throne with the Fat Duke. When the Little Vassal is on his own, he can make his body flat, shaped like a slice of bacon, and spread himself over the greatest area of the throne to provide his fellow townspeople with even more light. When the Fat Duke is present on the throne, however, he finds that if he is not quick enough, the Fat Duke sits on top of him, and he has to shape himself sitting upright like a piece of toast in a rack.*
>
> *There is a terrible scream from outside the room. People are shouting, "Douleur, frustration, cholère!" [pain, frustration, anger].*

This dream can be seen as an allegory, describing the state of the company with its power structure. The Fat Duke and the Little Vassal represent the share holding of the company's principal owners, with the townspeople as the smaller, private investors. The Fat Duke is German, the Little Vassal is French, though for reasons of confidentiality no further details can be given. The dream summarizes much of the feelings of frustration at being in this joint company, which publicly operated as a French company in reality. There would be joint marketing seminars and meetings. The pain, frustration, and anger is voiced by the managers through the dreams.

All the French managers thought that their company had the majority of shares—after all, the original companies, from which the present group had been structured, were indubitably French. The German–French axis was seen as being right, and fashionable, because old political and national enemies were now allies. It gave the total group, now a joint venture of both French and German businesses, a great deal of commercial power in a highly competitive market.

The mobile of the architect son was very original in the dream, but the Fat Duke disapproved. One of the complaints of the French managers was that the German managers always held sway in the marketing meetings. French ideas were always seen as lacking. The mobile, reminiscent of a DNA structure, was modelled like a double helix. The thought it provoked was that the future managers (architect sons of the Little Vassal) were struggling to give their companies a new identity and marketing stamp, symbolized by the mobile.

The Fat Duke and the Little Vassal sitting on the throne symbolized the hidden struggle between the Germans and the French. The Little Vassal could give light (leadership and employment), and it was assumed that with the aid of the Fat Duke this would be increased, but in fact the Fat Duke would squeeze out the Little Vassal from the throne (the symbol of power).

This dream gave expression to something that was known, but had never been thought publicly. It was a prescient dream. All the French managers believed that their nationality owned the majority shares, whereas in actuality it was owned by the Germans. This was contained in a secret clause. This is an example of the "unthought known" made conscious in a dream. Here we see the influence of systemic thinking. Thinking as being and becoming is influenced by the domain of thinking as dreaming and thinking as the unthought known relate to each other. To put this another way: here, conscious thinking is influenced by the domain of dreaming and the unconscious. Now people could be aware of something that had had to be hidden, or "not thought".

The infinite is present in the act of dreaming because the dreams introduce other dimensions to existence, expressed often in surreal images. The repeated mention of "faith" is another indication of the infinite in the sense of having faith not to know and be uncertain. The dreams present the facts of everyday life in another form, but in such a way that their real meaning can be discerned. As the dreams are recounted and the participants free-associate, the infinite becomes immanent; it begins to be in the participants' grasp, and not as something imagined to be transcendent. The infinite is the unknown, and the dream introduces us to this: it questions what we have assumed, and accepted, to be social knowledge.

As important is the fact that the dreams, of which we give a small sample from the totality, together with a small sample of the possible associations, gave expression to the experience of being a manager. The social dreaming matrix gave participants an opportunity to stand outside their company role, to reflect and to think afresh. They could have a range of emotions, like fun and sadder feelings, as they associated to the dreams, which were expanding their thinking.

A few weeks after the seminar, another dream was reported to the writer. One manager, who was due to take over the role of managing director of one of the companies in the group, had been recording his observations of the company in a notebook. He had been noting the issues he had to address and reasoning out the decisions he had to make. He had lost the notebook before the seminar, and his colleagues had commiserated with him on his loss.

The night after the seminar, he had a dream in which *he placed the notebook in the drawer of a black desk*. On waking, he thought of black desks. He did not have one, either in his office or in his home. The only one he knew of was the president's, but it was highly unlikely that he would have put his notebook there. As the manager thought of his notebook, he remembered that the desk had been an antique one, with a not very smooth top. He recalled that he had recently been in a hotel with such a desk. He telephoned the hotel, and the manager of the hotel said: "Yes, we have your notebook! We didn't know where to mail it, but we shall send it tomorrow." Social dreaming may be useful in finding the "lost properties" of our dreams.

Note

1. The terms "taker" and "host" were introduced later to describe the consultant role in social dreaming.

CHAPTER TWO

What is social dreaming?

The task of social dreaming is to transform thinking through exploring dreams, using the methods of free association, amplification, and systemic thinking, so as to make links and find connections in order to discover new thinking and thoughts.

What is meant by this?

The human ability to transform thinking has meant that daily life is different from five decades ago, and totally different from the time of the Romans, for example. Thinking is transformed in quite ordinary ways: a word is changed; a concept is rethought; an idea is developed; a poem is written; a work of art is created; a scientific law is formulated.

Thinking, and all associated creative and inventive endeavour, has its roots in the undifferentiated matrix of unconscious imagery. It underlies the conscious imagery we use every day of our lives.

The social dreaming matrix is a structured opportunity to share dreams with others. It is both a form and a process. As a form, it is a configuration of people that provides a unique space, or container, or receptacle for thinking of the content of dreams to consider and discover their hidden, infinite meaning. As a process, the matrix, which is explained below, is the system, or web, of emotions and thinking that is present in every social relationship but is unattended and not acknowledged, for the most part. The matrix mirrors the unconscious, or infinite, processes in waking life that give rise to dreaming when asleep.

In social dreaming the dreamers tell their dreams to others. Although individuals are necessary to dream the dreams, the dream itself is not just a personal possession, for it also captures the political and institutional aspects of the dreamers' social context and how these are present or laced into their struggles for creativity, meaning, and ordinariness. The meaning of the dream is expanded and developed through free association, amplification, and systemic thinking to give voice to the echoes of thinking and thought that exist in the space between individuals' minds in the shared environment.

Social dreaming on identifying the patterns that connect the various dreams reveals the underlying nature of the organization, of the society, and poses questions as to the social nature of dreaming.

Social dreaming makes possible a change from the traditional polarity of conscious ↔ unconscious to finite ↔ infinite because it alters the function of dreaming from being a therapeutic method of individual exploration of the unconscious to existing in the imaginative space of the dream in which all human culture and knowledge has its origins. The focus alters from the dreamer to the dream. Individuals taking part in social dreaming are relieved of the necessity to defend their private inner world as they engage in the cooperative venture of creating knowledge to understand the social milieu.

Consciousness can be understood to be subjectivity, which registers experiences of ourselves as human beings, based on emotions, feelings, and the resultant thinking and thought. In the context of the individual it makes sense to use the categories of the unconscious ↔ conscious dimensions of mind when thinking about personal issues.

By contrast, *social dreaming directs attention to shared culture and knowledge and takes us beyond personal, selfish, ego-centric preoccupations.* Social dreaming emphasizes the systemic, holistic quality of dreams and leaves aside the personal, which is to take an atomistic perspective. From social experience human beings make use of working hypotheses as a scientific method to attain this culture and knowledge. Social dreaming is derived from social experience. Therefore, in this context, the idea of finite ↔ infinite knowledge makes more sense because it is a shared concept and is potentially common to all individuals as more and more minds relate.

Dreams are related systemically, just as thinking is. Each dream is a fractal of the other, for dreaming is revealed in repeating patterns: one dream is part of a whole sequence of dreams in a matrix. Working with the potential meanings of dreams, we attempt to find the pattern that connects the dreams. Conventionally, as individuals, we would analyse the dreams, seeing them as separate entities, delving into the component parts of the dream as symbols, acting as detectives to identify the private, psychic dimensions of the life of the dreamer.

In social dreaming, the systemic thinking[1] method can be used to find a systems-wide focus: a more holistic viewpoint. This is a combination of analytical thinking and synthetic thinking. In analytical thinking things are broken down to their smallest component. But what is lost in that process is the capacity to see how everything interacts with everything else. Synthetic thinking tries to find the common themes as repeating patterns in a system or situation so as to find connections. Using the two, we arrive at systemic thinking. This is to identify the common themes and the patterns that connect them.

The immediate benefit of the social dreaming matrix is that thinking is expanded and transformed as the participants begin to recognize that new information is embedded in the dreaming. This is more effective than any conscious, finite scrutiny. As has been proven experimentally, the uncon-

> *scious, subliminal scanning powers of the unconscious/infinite are superior to conscious, rational vision. In social dreaming it becomes possible not only to link the conscious patterns, but also to identify and make explicit the unconscious ones. Social dreaming combines the use of the logic of consciousness and the non-logic of the unconscious. Thus, the patterns that connect finite thinking with what is in the infinite, or the not-known, are discerned.*

Social dreaming breaks with contemporary Western thinking on dreaming and dreams and harks back to a time when dreaming was part of the conversational discourse of everyday life: not secret and kept separate from others, denied, reviled, or discarded as useless, parasitic junk of the mind.

How can we as human beings discard dreams as useless when each night they beguile us with their mystery? How can we attempt to jettison our dreams, possessed of so much grandeur, charm, and terror? Dreams arise from the emotional state we are in when we go to sleep. This emotional state may be forgotten in our conscious memory, but it will be activated during sleep, while the unconscious is at work. During a dream we may not experience emotion, though we do so occasionally. It is in recounting the dream while awake that we become more aware of the emotion experienced in the dream.

When dream-life is rejected, we cut ourselves off from great swathes of the emotions and feelings of our unconscious life that inform so much of our consciousness—far more than can ever be credited.

Social dreaming has existed for as long as mankind has been on earth. Aborigines, and what were called in earlier centuries "primitive" tribes, had been using dreaming to inform their daily life. The evidence exists in the *Epic of Gilgamesh,* which was written down from oral tradition in the third millennium B.C. The Bible, the Koran, and many classics of world literature report dreams as illuminating the condition in which people lived, highlighting the dilemmas and problems faced and offering solutions. The dream was seen predominantly as a cultural phenomenon, not as a tool for understanding the psyche of the individual. Freud discovered this, but in focusing on the individual and the therapeutic dimension, the idea of the cultural and systemic qualities of dreaming was de-emphasized and came in danger of being lost.

Freud postulated that dreaming came from the "unconscious", which he made a central feature of his method. The unconscious exists as a subjective fact of the psyche. The mind, or psyche, produces dream-thinking and dreams. What is the mind? What do we need to know to understand its function in dreaming?

Note

1. There are a number of accounts of systemic thinking; on the Internet, the website www.probsolv.com has an excellent summary under the topic "concept".

CHAPTER THREE

The marvelling mind of humans

The mind, when asleep, gives rise to dreaming, which is a basic form of thinking. Without mind, with its capacity for thinking and thought, all the science, technology, art, philosophy, literature, and the social, political, economic, and spiritual processes that make for that collective cultural experience called civilization, would have no existence. Without the mind and thought, there would be no business enterprises, which are a defining feature of contemporary Western civilization. Someone, or a group of people, think of a business in the first instance. This idea they make into a real project. The business enterprise can only continue existing if the people most closely associated—both managers and employees—continue to think.

Mind has no material reality and is invisible, but it exists in our imagination. Neuroscience, the science of the brain, is attempting to produce a unified theory, and more and more is being discovered, but we know—as opposed to having informed, scientific opinions—comparatively little of the mind.

What is known is that the mind, at its best, can achieve greatness and the heights of creativity, and, at its worst, it can be the source of destruction, terror, and tragedy. The qualities of mind have been encapsulated by Christian De Duve:

> The mind generates our thoughts, reasoning, intuitions, ponderings, inventions, designs, beliefs, doubts, imaginings, fantasies, desires, intentions, yearnings, frustrations, dreams and nightmares. It brings up evocations of our past and it shapes plans for our future; it weighs, decides, and commands. It is the seat of consciousness, self-awareness, and personhood, the holder of freedom and moral responsibility, the judge of good and bad, the inventor and agent of virtue and sin. It is the focus of all our feelings, emotions and sensations, of pleasure and pain, love and hate, rapture and despair. The mind is the interface between what we are wont to call the world of matter and the world of spirit. The mind is our window to truth, beauty, charity and love, to existential mystery, the awareness of death, the poignancy of the human condition. [De Duve, 1995, p. 245]

Thinking about thinking and thought

Thinking is the process by which the mental image of the object of thought is manipulated independently in the imagination. Thinking can be of four kinds, or modes, it can be suggested. There is *thinking as being* (Lawrence, 2000b). This is the thinking about the human state and condition. This is the background thinking to all that we do. It is a bit like white noise; always present. To put this negatively: rare are the moments when we have no-thought going on in our minds.

But human beings are always thinking of ways to improve, or make progress, by imagining a future state and how they are to attain it. This can be termed *thinking as becoming*. For example, strategic planners in a business company are charged with working out what the future commercial survival of their company will be when the economy experiences a downturn. A simple example would be redecorating, in our minds and without getting out of the chair, the room in which we are presently sitting. Again, gardeners are thinking of what their garden could become next year, or a few years later. These two modes of thinking—being and becoming—tend to exist in the light of consciousness. We tend to be fully awake when we think of what we are and what we might become.

There are two other kinds of thinking—*thinking as dreaming* and *thinking as the "unthought known"* (Bollas, 1987)—which have their origins in the shadow-land of unconsciousness, or the infinite.

Thinking as dreaming is the way that human beings emotionally experiment with their daily actions while they are asleep. In this miraculous way they access their powerful unconscious life by accessing the infinite thinking that is present in their dreaming and culture. Consider the evolution of the single-cell organism, existing in ponds million of years ago, and how human beings have evolved. Could it be that this comes from these single cells engaging in some form of proto-dreaming to become what we now are?

Unthought knowns come to be registered in our inner world as a result of life events that will, when similar events are experienced subsequently, evoke a memory of the initial experience, which, in a sense, has been "forgotten". This stirring of memory causes thinking. So there is dredged up from our unconscious memory bank something that we knew but have never had the opportunity to think about. An example is shown in the "Fat Duke and Little Vassal" dream in chapter one.

Although these four modes of thinking have been made separate for exposition, they are systemically related as each of the modes interact with each other. This can be drawn as a plan of a four-sided pyramid (see Figure 1). The square base of the pyramid can be construed as the domains of thinking that use the knowledge of, for example, language, logic, philosophy, systems thinking, architecture, business management, and any of the sciences.

Clearly, the four modes are experiential and fluid by their nature. The domains are more of a recorded experience that has come to be enshrined, or codified, in culture and knowledge systems. The domains are more stable and static by nature,

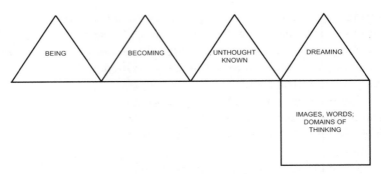

FIGURE 1:   The four modes of thinking.

though they will change through the experiences of the four modes of thinking. A useful distinction is that the four modes apply to thinking, whereas the domains of thinking are thoughts that have been enshrined as disciplines. The former are the present continuous tense, the latter the past.

Figure 1 shows a way of ordering our methods of thinking. It is not definitive by any means and may be simplistic, but it will serve as a basis for thinking about thinking and thought.

Science based on Newtonian physics was a comparatively stable body of knowledge until Einstein, Bohr, and other scientists discovered quantum reality and physics. A child born 70 year ago was taught science based on Isaac Newton. Now a child must not only be taught traditional science but must be aware of the new science. There is now a new paradigm of science that grew in the nineteenth and twentieth centuries. This illustrates how knowledge and science develop through the application of thinking and its resultant thought. The thinking that produced quantum physics took place in the interaction between and within the four modes of thinking, taking into account the existing scientific knowledge contained in the established domains of thought.

The capacities of the mind can be sharpened through the cultivation of a *mental disposition*. By this is meant the forging of an attitude of mind that is directed at discovery and is capable of registering wonderment and surprise. Apart from the development of intelligence, which can, loosely, be termed brain power, there is the authority of the mind.

By this is meant using the idea of authority, which has its roots in the mind. The paradox is that to author thinking, one needs a mind, but in that authorizing, the mind is further developed. This idea of the authority of the mind is critical for managing oneself in the context of all that the mind is capable of thinking. But minds do not exist in isolation, and what is being thought by other people with minds has also to be taken into account. So the idea of empathy is important. All this requires the courage to follow through the implications of thinking, no matter where they may lead.

To attain this mental disposition of developing the authority of the mind means cultivating the capacity for reverie and the capacity to be alone, which is linked to imaginative day-dreaming. This children possess in abundance, and it forms the basis of *autobiographical memory* (Schachtel, 2001), but it is gradually lost as children grow to adulthood. So, in a real sense, attaining this mental disposition is about rescuing this capacity from childhood.

Childhood, when the ability to be alone is discovered, is a period when children are full of questions and wonderment; however, as they learn through schooling and education, they acquire *useful memory*, and the early memories and the capacity for reveries slip away into the unconscious. The autobiographical memory is replaced by useful memory: the various schemata of knowledge that society deems to be of use in earning a living and being a citizen, which are essential for survival as an adult.

There is a real sense in which something of childhood wonderment is recaptured in dreaming because our autobiographical memory, even though lodged in the unconscious, remains with us forever and will revisit us in our dreaming until we die. Life has sleep stirred by dreams, but death is dreamless sleep. Dreaming and the capacity to listen to our dreams is one way to recapture the imaginative space of reverie with its wonderment and surprise, but, as important, it allows us to continue to cultivate the authority of our minds.

Speech, acquired by imitating adults, is the way that children learn how to represent their bodily wishes and thinking. Speech makes conscious thought possible by becoming associated to the unconscious thinking processes. So, running through the four modes of thinking (Figure 1), is speech, through which people communicate their unconscious thinking to make their experience conscious.

A simple example of the interaction between autobiographical and useful memory can be given in the writing of a poem: A scene in India was witnessed of men cutting rice using sickles. Sickles lead to the association of childhood memories of harvesting in the days of horse-drawn binders. To allow the binder access to cut the corn, a way had to be cleared around the edges of the field. This was done by a man using a scythe—a later and more efficient form of the sickle. In a flash, the writer was catapulted into a world he thought he had lost, but which was registered in a long-forgotten memory. Emotional images and the language of childhood were re-discovered. The speech of childhood—in this case, a Scottish dialect—was revisited as a defining part of autobiographical memory. This had been lost as useful memory had been acquired and subsequently rendered in English as a result of education. A for the most part forgotten grandfather was re-evoked, together with the feelings of that time. Tears flowed, because the memories belonged to a period when the writer was six years old: happy, secure, content. The first draft of the poem was written that evening.

Dreaming arises from the individual's psyche. Dreams are surreal, bizarre manifestations that in waking life it would be difficult imagine. These night-time constructions leave the dreamer bemused, as if he had been to the cinema. It is no wonder that dreams have an important role in the Bible and in ancient texts, like the *Epic of Gilgamesh*, already mentioned. The surreal, multifarious, bewildering form and content of dreams are put into a narrative order when awake and examined, but it is difficult to recapture the full experience of the dream.

This process of putting the dream into a narrative order is to make explicit the implicit content of the dream. This is the beginnings of the transformation of thinking. One dimension of human beings' sense of authority comes, it is being argued, from accessing dreams and struggling to make their implicit, mysterious, entangled images and words explicit by unfolding their meanings. This process is continued until some version of the truth of the dream is attained.

The individual psyche exists in an environment—or eco-niche—that presents existential puzzles about the nature and quality of that environment, coupled with the place of human beings in it. These puzzles fuel dreams. By engaging in the task of understanding dreaming, their implicit meaning becomes clearer as the dreams are transformed into words that yield their ultimate explicit meaning. When this shared by a collection of people, there are many more resources for addressing the images, doubts, uncertainties, and truths embedded in the mystery of the dreams. Social dreaming is one of the methods of transforming thinking and is, therefore, a sure way of cultivating the capacities of the mind.

The process of dreaming and making the implicit explicit, starting from the "black hole of the psyche" and ending in words and meaning, is captured by Montague Ullman (1975; see Figure 2).

Imagine what takes place when there are between 6 and 30 people giving their dreams and thinking about them, which is what happens in a social dreaming matrix.

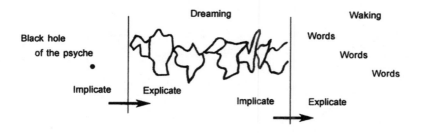

FIGURE 2:   Dreaming and making explicit the implicit
(from Ullman, 1975, p. 9).

Some basic notions having been outlined, a number of ideas on the conscious and the unconscious, on the finite and the infinite are presented in chapter four. To build an emergent theory, actual examples of social dreaming are then given in subsequent chapters.

The underestimated value of unconscious thinking

Obviously, social dreaming involves the unconscious mind, its processes, and how dream thinking and images can be transformed into consciousness.

Most people believe that they manage themselves in their various roles by exclusively using their consciousness and finite knowledge. This is impossible, because the bandwidth of consciousness that is the basis for our decision-making uses only 18 bits of information per second. (A "bit" is weightless, colourless, has no size, and can travel at the speed of light: "It is the smallest atomic element in the DNA of information"—Negroponte, 1995). The bandwidth of consciousness is too narrow to process the 14 million bits of information we routinely receive and act on to survive as organisms in the world. This enormous gap is filled by unconscious information: communal knowledge that is of the infinite, that we routinely use to make decisions and to take action. It is humbling to recognize that we have conscious access to roughly a millionth of the information we need to exist as organisms (Gray, 2002).

Infinite, unconscious information can be accessed through dreaming. This is a remarkable but underused ability of human beings. In the cinema of the night, when we are asleep, we take part in adventures that we could barely imagine when awake. We are in a surreal dream-place that is out of time and space. This space is not controlled by our conscious, ratiocinating mind whose functions are temporarily suspended in sleep.

When we dream, we find ourselves on speaking terms with our unconscious mind: with the infinite. Throughout this book, the unconscious and the infinite are understood to be potentially enabling and creative, not to be feared and so rejected or denied or disparaged.

We can understand ourselves as having two lives: our waking life of consciousness, and our life of sleeping and dreaming. We dream to make sense of the experiences of our waking life. In the dream we are thinking how to understand, react, and adapt to the environment we occupy. The dream is an imaginative replay of our state of being in our social world and a rehearsal of how we are to become in relation to our environment. The images that come to us through dreaming become the patterns that we live by. If we cannot recognize the pattern, we condemn ourselves to living without insight. By recognizing these patterns, we live more fully as human beings, better able to manage ourselves in our roles (Lawrence, 1999).

If we accept the positive aspects of the unconscious, we enhance the quality of our consciousness. In actuality, the conscious mind and the unconscious mind are in a symbiont relationship, with one relying on the other for its existence. If the information from the unconscious mind is made absent from our thinking, we curtail our ability to use our conscious mind and intelligence as a totality. The finite ↔ infinite are in constant interaction, sustaining each other. Dreaming and dream-work are indications of both the presence and the absence of our human experience. Mind is not an identifiable entity: it is a process.

Whereas the conscious mind operates on the basis of logical, repeated patterns of thinking, the unconscious mind uses a totally different logic by working on analogues. We can never fully know what is unconscious, as its name implies; but we do recognize that the unconscious is always in a state of becoming as it makes its insight and information felt as a presence to be recognized in consciousness.

The logic of the unconscious, or infinite, is based on symmetry. It tends to fuse and unite everything in a oneness that is limitless. In contradistinction, the scientific thinking of everyday life works within a framework of distinguishing things. The infinite is the realm of the illogical (Freud, 1900a).

Dreams are timeless. Real and imaginary events have the same validity, just as assertions and their negation are identical in the dream. Furthermore, logical connections are reproduced in the dream as being simultaneous. These were among some of the characteristics of dreams as Freud first identified them (Freud, 1900a).

We know that:

> Unconscious vision . . . [has] proved to be capable . . . of gathering more information than a conscious scrutiny lasting a hundred times longer . . . the undifferentiated structure of unconscious vision . . . displays scanning powers that are superior to conscious vision. [Ehrenzweig, 1967, p. 63]

Unconscious vision provides us with subliminal perceptions of the reality in which we have our being and existence, and in which we make a living. Dreaming is the human way to access the unconscious, with its unique logic. By making the patterns of dreaming part of our waking life, we enhance the bandwidth of consciousness and so have a greater capacity for processing information.

What is made conscious has been "Won from the void and formless infinite" (Milton) (Symington, & Symington, 1996). This reformulation of the conscious ↔ unconscious polarity to finite ↔ infinite best fits what the social dreaming matrix is designed to capture. The infinite has no form, no categories, no number, and is the domain of what we do not know. The finite is what we know. The transforming process by means of dreaming is one way that the infinite passes into finite grasp. Of the infinite—that which is beyond our immediate ken—every human being has an inkling. Consciousness of the finite grows, just as the mind grows, through resonating with and trying to understand the infinite. Throughout this monograph, however, we use these terms: "unconscious", meaning the personal unconscious; and "infinite" for the social unconscious when congeries and groups of people resonate with each other and become a shared experience. The infinite, which I use in the poetical rather than mathematical sense, is only apprehended occasionally in the course of a SDM.

Einstein outlined the thinking processes for understanding the infinite that led to his discoveries of quantum physics. Words and language did not play any role in the mechanism of thought. He started from images of physical entities and vaguely played with them. This combinatory play, he wrote, seemed to be an essential feature of productive thought, occurring before any logical constructions in words or other signs. This play is aimed to be analogous to the logical connections he is searching for. Then he searches for words. He follows this path to arrive at mathematical formulations. To summarize: he starts from an emotional state expressed in images and sensations to lead him to purely intellectual and highly abstract conceptions. In short, he is saying that emotion is the mother of thinking, while the unconscious is the father. The indivisible oneness of the infinite is present in all our lives and is the background to everything that exists. The heterogeneity of scientific thought and classical logic attempts, perhaps desperately, to "get inside" the nature of this indivisible wholeness, to bring it into its own realm of the scientific based on the divisible and heterogeneity. But all this begins from emotion and feelings, as Einstein readily acknowledged.[1]

Note

1. Matte-Blanco sets out his radical formulation of the unconscious in *The Unconscious as Infinite Sets* (1975) and *Thinking, Feeling, and Being* (1988).

CHAPTER FIVE

The differences of consciousness in relation to the unconscious

As humans, we can give meaning to the cosmos because we possess consciousness, or self-awareness. If there were no life in the cosmos, it would be a meaningless void. Because there is life, it has a meaning, which will be expanded over time as human beings learn, question, and develop new working hypotheses to make new meaning.

For example, in the sixteenth century, through his use of the newly developed telescope, Galileo was able to observe the sun, the moon, and the planets. Based on the scientific work of Copernicus, he showed that the earth moved, but the sun was constant. This scientific finding went against the faith of the Catholic Church, which had made it doctrine that the earth was the centre of the universe. Despite the scientific evidence, Galileo was subjected to an Inquisition, and the Church's view prevailed. The Establishment won out against the genius of Galileo, but in the long term it was the meaning that Galileo gave to the place of the sun in the universe that has entered scientific discourse as a fact.

This is an example of how the meaning of the universe is revealed to mankind as a result of man's consciousness and self-awareness that questions the nature of the environment that surrounds human beings.

This self-awareness or consciousness starts from the human brain. The brain, in turn, produces mind. Put simply, the brain is the physical hardware that operates to produce the mind and its functioning. Mind could not exist without the prior existence of the brain, but brain can exist without the mental processing of the mind.

The cortex of the brain, according to neurobiologists, consists of many billions of neurons, which configure as "neural nets". These nets of the mind have been mapped using computers. What happens when we are awake and conscious is that these nets are connected very tightly and are very focused. To do reading, writing, and arithmetic (the three R's), we rely on these nets being closely bound together, as we do for all scientific thinking.

When we are asleep and in a not-conscious state, the situation changes in the nets of the mind. Sleep researchers have found that there are two activities during sleep—Rapid Eye Movement (REM) and non-REM—the former when we dream and more in touch with our unconscious, the latter more like the state when we are awake and still able to make use of our tightly knit nets of the mind. In particular when we are engaged in REM sleep, there are further changes in the nets of the mind: they dissolve and become less tightly knit, with the connections becoming loose and broader.

The dream being the royal road to the unconscious, to use Freud's celebrated phrase, it is possible to find the limits of the conscious and the unconscious mind through dreaming. The mind can be seen as a functioning whole, with two symbiont parts—the conscious and unconscious—each relying on the other for the whole of mind to function. There are no fixed boundaries between these two parts: rather, there are limits that will be different for each person, but there is implicit consensus among people as to what they are.

Variable	Focused waking thought	Looser, less-structured waking thought	Reverie, free association, daydreaming	Dreaming
What dealt with?	Perceptual input: math symbols, signs, words	Fewer words, signs; more visual-spatial imagery		Almost pure imagery
How?	Logical relationship: if A then B	Less logic, more noting or picturing of similarities, more metaphor		Almost pure picture metaphor
Self-reflection	Highly self-reflective: "I know I am sitting here reading"	Less self-reflective; more "caught up" in the process, the imagery		In "typical dreams" total *thereness*, no self-reflection
Sequence of ideas or images	A→B→C→D	A→B→C, D	A→B→C, D	(diamond) A, B, C, D
Processing	Relatively serial; net functions chiefly as a feed-forward net		Net functions more as an autoassociative net	
Boundaries	Solid division, categorization, thick boundaries	Less rigid categorization, thinner boundaries		Merging, condensation; loosening of categories; thin boundaries
Subsystems	Activity chiefly *within* structured subsystems		Activity less *within*, more *across* or *outside* structured subsystems	

FIGURE 3:   A wake–dreaming continuum (Hartmann, 2000, p. 67).

It is possible to map the consensual limits between consciousness and the unconscious, between waking life and dream-life, between 3R thinking and activity and what is not. Hartmann (2000) has drawn up such a table (see Figure 3).

This illustrates how the mind works with thinking and thought. In the conscious mind the nets of the mind are tightly structured. Consequently, the sequence of ideas are linear: thought follows thought logically. When the unconscious is operating, the mental nets of the mind are looser, and so thinking is branching and is auto-associative. This is ultimate free association. The thinking follows its own free-will, so to speak.

Boundaries and subsystems of knowledge are more rigidly adhered to in the conscious mind. But this is far less so when the unconscious holds sway. The boundaries are less defined, cat-egories are loosened, and there is thinking activity both outside and across the subsystems of knowledge.

The conscious and the unconscious are not rigid categories but are merged in the continuum of the mind. The unconscious can be seen as the source of creativity (and destruction), for it puts into disarray the cultural schemata we live by and, there-fore, questions the neat, logical categories of our mental lives.

In a brilliant paper called "The Undifferentiated Matrix of Artistic Imagination", Anton Ehrenzweig (1964) puts forward the notion that underlying the conscious imagery of art, there exists an "unconscious undifferentiated imagery", and a true artist makes use of this in producing a work of art.

In an attempt to be more efficient, every company system develops a bureaucratic organization. This may range from mild to severe: the more severe the bureaucracy, the more the system is governed by rational madness, for the management are anx-ious to control. Boundaries are rigid and feel like prisons. Every system experiences the struggle between managerial control and the degree of freedom required for everyone to manage themselves in their role.

To break up this rigidity of thinking and thought, a manage-ment could initiate social dreaming matrices for both senior managers and their employees. The chances of creativity in the company organization being enhanced would be increased. A matrix could be set up on an hour-a-week basis, for example. To help in this, some basic ideas on how to organize a matrix are given in appendix 1.

CHAPTER SIX

Working with the social dreaming matrix

As work has proceeded with the social dreaming matrix, some basic concepts have had to be evolved. Five terms have to be given meaning in the context of social dreaming:

- working hypothesis
- matrix
- free association
- amplification
- systemic thinking.

Working hypothesis

The working hypothesis is a sketch of reality, an approximation, as it is perceived. On further testing of reality, the working hypothesis will be confirmed or will be seen as redundant because the evidence does not match the perceived reality. Then another working hypothesis can be substituted. This process will be continued until the most adequate maps are construed between the perception of reality and the working hypothesis.

This scientific method is used in everyday life. Each of us learns from experience, which is registered emotionally but periodically *reaches the limits of our comprehension* of the nature of the reality being experienced. A successful company starts to make a loss. The management try every way they can to attain profit, but they are not successful. One hypothesis is that they have reached the limits of comprehension of their market. They know the logic of their business that has brought success in the past, but the logic no longer matches the demands of the environment. Their finite world of knowledge is being challenged by infinite knowledge. They no longer know, and they begin to acquire the courage to foster the ability not to know.

Once this is recognized, they begin to reflect on what has hitherto been the infinite. They use their ability to use their unconscious scanning powers. They think of their market, which has changed because of the changing aspirations of their customers. They begin to study their market afresh and make working hypotheses as to which products will sell best. As a result they innovate and make changes to their product and marketing. They begin to have success.

Reaching the limits of finite comprehension, not-knowing, is the beginnings of wresting knowledge from the infinite. All scientific discoveries arise from scientists reaching the point where they do not understand the phenomena they are investigating. The breakthrough to new knowledge comes when this is recognized. They make use of their unconscious mind, unwittingly or purposefully, to formulate working hypotheses. The answer to their problem may come in a creative insight, but it is likely to come in a dream.

The chemist Kekule, to use an oft-cited example, was trying to solve the problem of the molecular structure of benzene. He had worked on the problem for years. One afternoon he took a nap, and he had a dream of *a writhing snake eating its own tail*. The dream showed him that the structure of this organic compound might be a closed ring. Kekule had solved the problem through dreaming. The illumination of the problem through the dream came after a long period of preparation, while Kekule had made working hypotheses, tested them, and found them wanting. Going to sleep that afternoon was a period of incubation for Kekule, which resulted in the illuminating dream. All that remained was to verify his results empirically.

Can we say that the dream is a figment of the unconscious imagination, which plumbs the infinite while asleep to wrestle with the working hypotheses arrived at as we encounter the daily issues and problems of our lives?

Matrix

> *The matrix is the name of the space in which social dreaming takes place; it is composed of people, numbering, say, 6 to 60, who meet for the purpose of using free association on the dreams given to the matrix by participants. The aim is to make links and find connections among the dreams. This relies on the thinking of the participants.*

The matrix is used to capture the space of thinking and free associations. It is a space that mirrors, while awake, the space of dreaming while asleep, giving rise to images, metaphors, analogues, and symbols. The matrix symbolizes the space between mothers and babies where thinking has its origin in the cultural space between them. It is also a representation of the infinite, of not knowing.

The matrix as thinking space and the origins of thought is also an attempt to mobilize the unconscious images and symbols that inform our conscious thinking. Matrix is the "container" of societies, groups and organizations in that it contains all the thought that has brought them into being and sustains them in their continuing existence. To achieve logical tasks, groups and organizations were first devised by humankind to bring about civilization. In that process, however, they simplified, regularized, and logically codified human behaviour so that it could be "contained". Therefore, it submerged, or screened out, infinite thought.

Matrix is also to experience a democratic environment. Why? Free association means saying what comes to mind; it is not subject to rational control. Free associations are non-judgemental, so there is a sense of liberty. The thinking that results is surprising and synchronous. This is because social dreaming is conducted in a matrix, not a group.

Matrix has other connotations. All living systems are biologically made of cells. These cells develop metabolism, which is the continuous chemistry that enables the cell to maintain itself as a living being. Metabolism is the taking in of nutrients, allowing the cell to maintain itself. This chemical action gives rise to autopoiesis: that continual re-making of itself that every living thing goes through. This is the criterion for distinguishing between living and non-living systems.

From single-cell organisms, the story of evolution unfolds. One feature of the story is symbiosis: the tendency of organisms to live in close association with each other (Capra, 1997) or even inside one another, like the bacteria in our intestines. These symbiont relationships have been of crucial importance for evolution.

What is a constant of evolution is the fact that all these processes—and here only the bare minimum have been indicated—are joined together in ecological networks, which communicate as systems and drive the evolutionary process.

> Driven by the creativity inherent in all living systems, expressed through the avenues of mutation, gene trading and symbiosis, and honed by natural selection, the planetary web of life expanded and complexified into forms of ever-increasing diversity. [Capra, 2002, p. 27]

Each matrix that is convened for social dreaming calls on this evolutionary story by tapping into the thinking processes that are integral to the web of thinking that has created the universe.

The participants in the matrix come to recognize that it is part of a universe-wide network of thinking that is directed at making and testing knowledge of the universe. What is known of the universe can only be so because of the existence of "knowers". If the universe were not inhabited by human beings, it would be an unknown and invisible universe (Greenstein, 1988). The universe needs living beings to experience and think of it—indeed, to think it into existence.

The matrix is a system and, like all systems, is exposed to our questioning.

> Systems thinking involves a shift from objective to "epistemic" science. This is a transition to a framework in which the generating of knowledge from the method of questioning, using subjectivity, becomes an integral part of scientific theories. [Capra, 1997, p. 40]

The working hypothesis arrived at in formulating the idea of social dreaming was that if it was to be conducted in a group, the people involved would become preoccupied with the "dynamics of the group". They would be caught up in the relationships between the participants. They would focus on the dreamers. The group would have reduced the logic of the potential thinking processes of the matrix by casting them in an asymmetrical mode. We wanted to get inside the symmetrical logic of the infinite.

To launch social dreaming and to be able to explore dream, it was necessary to unlearn all that was known of group and to create a feeling and thinking space—matrix—which would be open-ended. A matrix exists to explore what only a matrix can explore. To "see" what was in matrix, one had to be temporarily "blind" to what was known of group. The paradox is that the information of the infinite transcends and includes the information of group, but in being absorbed by the secondary processes and thinking of group, one is precluded from engaging with the primary, unconscious, infinite processes of matrix.

A pertinent analogy is that of the Faraday Cage: an earthed metal screen, invented by Michael Faraday, to insulate his experiments from electrostatic interference. There is a Faraday

Cage that has been constructed, in the mind, around the matrix, keeping it free from the interference of group dynamics and classical psychoanalysis, except where these have been tested in the processes of the matrix.

A group is an arena for individuals to pursue a primary task and to exercise their sense of purpose and their needs for power and security—at its worst, in a finite world dominated by task achievement. The matrix, on the other hand, is a collection of minds opening and being available for dwelling in possibility. It demands a different kind of leadership—one inspired by the recognition of the infinite, of not-knowing, of being in doubt and uncertainty, as opposed to knowing and repeating banal facts.

Plato in *Timaeus* (c. 360 BC) talks about the "receptacle" as a form of reality. The dialogue sets forth the idea that one form of reality is the world as "an intelligible and unchanging model and on the other a visible and changing copy of it". These, it is being postulated, are the infinite world and the finite world that human beings are constantly in a process of coming to know. The transformation from infinite to finite occurs in the "receptacle" that is the nurse of all becoming and change. Following this analogy, it is being postulated that "matrix" is the contemporary term for "receptacle", which is invisible and formless and possessed of intelligibility in a most puzzling way yet is hard to grasp. It remains constant because it never alters its characteristics, for it never changes, irrespective of what enters it. The receptacle is a place for the meeting of minds that can dwell in possibility. It can be added that in a receptacle the unconscious is very much in the foreground, with "group" and "system", which are conscious constructs, very much in the background.

Group, system, and related concepts only began to capture the imagination of people in the eighteenth and nineteenth centuries, with the important discoveries of group being made in the twentieth century, as modern civilization began to mobilize its imagination. Indeed, it can be argued that group and system that mobilize conscious thought will, on occasion, be used as a defence against the more unconscious thinking in the meeting of minds in the receptacle. Social dreaming was designed to mobilize unconscious thinking to mirror dream-life, Hence, matrix, it was hypothesized, provided the best container for encouraging unconscious imagery to be voiced.

What we know of the universe had its beginnings in the matrix of unconscious thinking and no-thinking that mankind first experienced millions of years ago. This thinking was first voiced, it can be conjectured, in the receptacle that Plato describes. The thinking became thought and entered the culture and knowledge of mankind. Now, the thought that constitutes the universe and is embedded in its very nature is available to living entities if they can question it and think to know. It would be impossible to guess how much knowledge remains unknown in the infinite, but scientists are gradually wresting information from the infinite to make it part of the domain of finite knowledge.

Recently, scientists using the Hubble Space Telescope and the Keck Telescope have discovered a new galaxy as the most distant object ever observed in the universe. This galaxy is so old that its light started its journey to earth when the universe was in its infancy, just 750 million years after the Big Bang. This illustrates, again, how knowledge is being wrested from the unknown by using scientific methods. What has hitherto been in the infinite is now part of finite knowledge.

Dreaming is the unconscious–infinite questioning process as we fathom the cultural puzzles with which we are presented throughout life. The worldwide system of dreaming, which goes on every second of life in the social unconscious of which the personal unconscious is a contributing element, is available for dreamers in search of a dream.

The matrix is also a space for reverie and day-dreams and aspects of play. Robert Louis Stevenson, the novelist, would make up stories on the basis of his day-dreams while playing with his toys as a child. Later he learned to use his night dreams. The writing of *The Strange Case of Dr Jekyll and Mr Hyde* (1886) came directly from a dream. He had been racking his brains for a story. On the second night he dreamed the scene of *Mr Hyde at the window, taking the powder and changing before his pursuers' eyes*. The rest of the story was worked out when Stevenson was awake and conscious.

In reverie and day-dreaming we slip from full consciousness and enter a state between the finite and infinity, able to let our minds roam in a free-associative fashion. The matrix enshrines this culture of play because it is non-judgemental and accepting of ideas.

Free association

> *Freud discovered free association with his patients. He used the metaphor of a train journey to describe it: As we look out of the window, each feature of the landscape lets loose impressions and thoughts that are free associations. To pass a church might give rise to the feeling that one has not been in such a place for decades, may remind one of an adolescent wish to be a Church minister, may cause one to reflect on the mystery of life, to consider the place of religion in the drive for colonization, may give rise to thinking of the role of Liberation Theology in the twentieth-century Roman Catholic Church, to consider how frail the Pope is, and so on.*

To free associate is to surrender oneself to trains of thought, without monitoring them for importance, relevance, or whether they are nonsense or disagreeable. Free association is a subversive activity that undermines "the entire structure of Western epistemology" (Bollas, 1991).

Our route to knowledge tends to be linear and rationally governed. Free association breaks up these thought processes, for it gives up the rational and discovers "truth by abandoning the effort to find it and adopting instead the leisurely task of stating what cross the mind from moment to moment" (Bollas, 2002). One set of associations to a dream will let loose other free associations. There are potentially as many free association as there are members of the matrix, leading to the matrix becoming a multi-verse of meanings, and with the participants managing themselves in their matrix role to make sense of the dream on their own authority.

Social dreaming depends on free association and amplification to fulfil its primary purpose.

Amplification

> *Jung discovered amplification, which means the enlarging of a thought, or a proposition, or an image. Amplification respects the integrity of the dream. Amplification is what participants naturally do when they listen to or offer a dream. They are looking for resemblances in the culture that has produced the particular dream. They will use their imagination by speculating on the social significance of the dream and freely associating along these lines. They will be puzzling about the symbolism of a particular word. They will each be coming up with answers, speculations, and guesses, in the context of their culture. In social dreaming this is all grist to the mill of the primary task, which is the transformation of thinking. There will be no wrong or right answer— just one idea that will lead to another, one dream that is extended in the next dream.*

Systemic thinking

> *In systemic thinking used with dreaming, one is looking for the pattern that connects the dreams:*
>
> *1. one lists all the system elements in the dreams;*
> *2. similar elements are grouped together by extracting the ideas contained in each group of elements;*
> *3. from these, the common themes are identified.*

In analytic thinking we tend to select the most promising themes, and we tend to discard the less promising ones—though clearly this is not so in psychoanalysis. We then select the best option, as we see it. Action plans are made on the basis of this selection. Systemic thinking looks at all the opportunities, using analytic thinking and systems thinking in concert, not in opposition (Lawrence, 1998b).

CHAPTER SEVEN

Social dreaming
as it illuminates political realities

C hance, fate, and intimations of destiny are apparent
in the political life of Israel, as in any nation state.
Social dreaming can bring these to the attention of
dreamers, as indications of the infinite. They can be con-
verted, of course, into private, therapeutic dreaming, which
takes attention away from the raw political issues that are
being illumined in the dreaming.

These political issues were voiced in Israel. But, first, it is essential to distinguish between social dreaming and what we have
called therapeutic dreaming.

Social dreaming is complementary to therapeutic dreaming.
Since the time of Freud, most investigation of dreaming has
fallen into the domain of psychoanalysis. This takes place in the
pair—or dyadic—situation of psychoanalyst and analysand. The
other possible situation is a group convened for psychotherapy.

This chapter is based in part on Lawrence & Biran (2002).

These therapeutic methods start from the assumption that the private troubles of the individual are important for resolution. By contrast, social dreaming starts from a different premise: the public issues of a milieu, society, or enterprise merit investigation and possible solutions because these affect the entire human environment. Obviously, the two approaches are complementary. One is not better than the other, but just different in its orientation. To summarize the differences:

Therapeutic dreaming	Social dreaming
Dreamer is the centre of attention	*Dream is the centre of attention*
The individual aspect	*The social aspect*
Egocentric orientation	*Socio-centric orientation*
Self-knowledge issues	*Gaining knowledge of the environment and its culture*
Dramatizing personal biography	*Facing the unpredictable, comic, and tragic aspects of being*

To put these two methods of working with dreaming into perspective, the idea of figure and ground can be used. In therapeutic dreaming the dreamer-as-person is the figure, with knowledge as the ground. In social dreaming the dream-as-knowledge is the figure, while self-understanding is the ground.

A dream in Israel was offered in a social dreaming matrix for researchers in organizations. The dream was of *a bizarre game in which the dreamer had one eye made of plastic or rubber. He would take it out, play with it, and put it back in place.* The associations were to the eye that sees and the eye that has impaired functioning. It was also about the limitation of vision, about half the picture that remains not seen.

If the dream had been recounted in a therapeutic situation, the chances are that the focus would have been on the aspects of punishment and castration, with the parts of the dreamer's life that he cannot see at this moment in time, with the nature of the psychic pain, which the dream had turned into play.

Since the dream was narrated in a social dreaming matrix, the dreamer was, perhaps, being warned through the dream of the danger of *hubris*, of being omniscient, of seeing and knowing all. He was being reminded of the limitations of vision and of the parts of him that are blind to experience and thinking about experience, as well as of the limitations of organizational consultancy. At the same time, since the dreamer belonged to a consultancy company, what was being indicated was the nature of the relationship between consultants and their organization. Was the consultant/researcher devalued in the organization by having his consulting eye turned into an artificial and useless organ?

The differences between therapeutic dreaming and social dreaming can be further illustrated. The dreamer was an observant Jewish settler in the Occupied Territories. Once the peace process is complete, it is possible that the residents in the settlements will have to leave their homes and move to communities inside Israel. The dreamer said that she had woken from the dream in terror.

> *I'm driving my car on the way to visit my two sons, who live near Haifa. I'm driving up a hill. I meet two other children, who live elsewhere. I realize that my family is scattered in different places around the country. I'm telling my two sons: "Don't keep on going, because we will not reach Haifa. The Sabbath is about to begin, and I will not ride the car on the Sabbath." My children show me a caravan near the road, and I decide to spend the Sabbath there. The children ease my mind, telling me that everything is fine. But I keep thinking, how come two of my children are here and two are there? I'm asking myself: Where am I? What happened to my home? Why am I not at home?*

I woke up with the question: where is our home?

Had this dream been told in a therapeutic group, the agenda would probably have concentrated on the dreamer's private life, her relations with her family members, or the experience of being uprooted from her permanent home as part of her personal history and conflict. What might also have been explored by the therapist could be what it is that is fragile in her inner world at the moment and how she is preparing for the changes in her life. Therapeutic thinking would have revolved around the strengthening of her ego to anticipate the changes coming her way.

The social dreaming matrix looks at much the same dream material but presented in a form suitable for a matrix. The other participants freely associated to this dream. The material that ensued consisted of associations that were to do with the human experience of being uprooted from the familiar, the fear of losing a home and of families breaking up, of human life being transient, unstable, of being the victim of chance. The dream brought up other dreams that were about family, generations, roots, belonging, security, emigration, moving from place to place, unanticipated changes in familiar scenery, refugees, survival, and so on.

In the social dreaming matrix the individual dream is no longer a personal, private possession; it is a representation of human fate, the unknown, and the insecurity of existence. It becomes an exploration of the knowledge by which we live our lives. The context of the dreamer's life becomes the narrative text of the matrix.

The dream is like one piece of a jigsaw puzzle that contains a multidimensional world. There are at least three additional ways of regarding the dream:

1. Concentrating on the *knowledge dimension* of the dream, we find information for the future in the caravan scene. The caravan is a symbol of the moving house. The dream is giving information about what is outside our field of vision, beyond our ken. Is it saying something about our changing, evolving world, about what will become? Living in a caravan may hint at transience, a world of easy mobility, even Internet surfing. It seems that the human psyche will have to adapt to more and more impermanent situations, which will span shorter periods of time. The element of chance and risk are present. Something in this dream arrests the familiar and stable

routines of life. The change is experienced as catastrophic. Are we being told that future life will be less rooted than the past and more exposed to temporary structures?

2. Another way is to use the *reverse perspective* on the dream. Something is going to happen to Jewish settlers; something raises alarm and concern in the society. But, paradoxically, it points to what is happening in reality to the Palestinian people. It is a mirror image, reflecting the fate of the refugees who have left their land and have spent long years in temporary houses in camps. The dreamer dreams that which had already happened to the other people—the breaking up of families, the exile from their land. If we look at this dream as shedding light on one half of the picture while keeping the other half in shadow, we may experience some of the human tragedy of the other.

3. There is a third perspective here: a pattern can be seen to the dreams in the matrix, but usually only with hindsight. This is the *meta-communication of the dreams*—that is, communication about communication. Currently, the events in Israel are terrifying: for the first time, the Jewish–Israeli population is being attacked by the Arab–Israeli one, but the Jewish–Israelis have more sophisticated weapons. The result is that the Arabs who live in cities and villages of Israel and who have Israeli citizenship are joining in spirit the Palestinians who live in the Territories. Former neighbours and places are becoming hostile and threatening. This issue for both Jew and Arab is: "Where is home?"

These are examples of the multidimensional aspects of dreaming. We cannot perceive all the dimensions, or all the perspectives, but only a small part of the infinity reflected in the dream. Further vignettes of political dreams from that country:

a. *I came back to the neighbourhood of my childhood. I visited the places in which I had played and had fun with my friends. But in my dream there was no fun. I felt terrified. The familiar place was not familiar any longer.*

b. *I visited my grandmother's home: a kind of visit that I always anticipate very much. But when I was inside her house, a group of people tried to enter the house, with the intention of hurting us. We hid. We were very frightened and were waiting for an opportunity to escape.*

c. *I am running and running and running, but my feet stay in the same place and I'm making no progress. I feel as if my feet are petrified. A group of strangers follow me. They are going to kill me.*

The significance of these dreams could not be discerned till the latest attempt to subjugate the Palestinians occurred in 2000. Leaders are under pressure by the superpowers to make political peace, but Palestinians and Israelis have reached the limits of tolerance. The dreams are the products of mutually distrustful cultures and point to the failure of rationally inspired debate in the peace process. This will continue until the raw fear and primitive social persecutory fears and anxieties, as expressed in the dreams, are addressed.

> *In social dreaming one has to be vigilant to ensure that finite knowledge, gained from classical psychoanalytic thought or from the study of groups and relationships, does not swamp the infinite insights of the matrix. The differences between therapeutic dreaming and social dreaming need to be celebrated, for each method investigates, accesses, and makes use of different kinds of understanding.*

CHAPTER EIGHT

Social dreaming, quantum reality, and the digital age

The argument has been that social dreaming illuminates social realities and their paradoxes. Dream-work is continuous day and night, and it operates on the receipt of stimuli that arise within and outside the psyche. The dream, experienced during sleep, is a mental, ideational product of the dream-work that is always taking place, even when we are fully awake.

Minds communicate with each other through language and speech. The growth of language is the experience of articulating the unknown that is implicit in the known. The poet and the dreamer have the same task, which is to convey experience through language that is "simple, sensuous and passionate" as Milton expressed it. Simile, metaphor, metonymy, synecdoche, and all the other figures of speech are used as the dreamer struggles in the day-to-day world to give a sense of having been in the transcendent world of the night, with its dreams. These figures of speech are the ways whereby the sense of the infinite is conveyed in common discourse. In dreaming, we each discover the difference between thoughts from the past, thinking of the present, and hitherto unknown thoughts that lie beyond the horizon of consciousness.

Every communication has both an explicit and implicit meaning. Within the explicit meaning there is embedded another set of meanings that are implicit. Contained in the explicit, manifest, logical thinking of everyday discourse, there is a rich stream of implicit thought and meaning. So, working out the meanings of dreams is a continual movement between a range of polarities: the explicit and the implicit, the finite and the infinite, the conscious and the unconscious, the transcendent and the immanent.

When Freud published *The Interpretation of Dreams* (1900a), he was leading the exploration into a mental territory that most people did not take seriously. Dreaming belonged to a world of the past, to mythology, to folklore, to fairy stories, to superstition. By 1900 the Western world was governed by the materialistic thinking that had brought about industrialization. The application of rational, logical, mechanical principles to the means of production was yielding tangible benefits to mankind, so why bother about intangible dreams?

Freud linked free association to dreaming and anticipated the digital age by contributing to the conditions that have brought it about. Free association breaks the sequence and continuity of thought processes to reveal hidden strands of thinking. It finds the implicit embedded in the explicit. It is an outcome of the essential subjectivity of individuals. Free association undermines the hegemony of logical and positivist thought.

Free association is of the essence of the digital age. The printed book, with its sentences, paragraphs, and chapters, follows sequentially in an order constructed by the author and dictated by the physical arrangement of the book. It is confined to three dimensions.

In the digital world, information space becomes enlarged to four dimensions. Every expression of ideas or train of thought also includes a network of pointers, which can be invoked or set aside.

A text can be seen as a complex molecular model:

> Chunks of information can be reordered, sentences ex-
> panded, and words given definition on the spot. . . . These
> linkages can be embedded either by the author at 'publish-
> ing' time or later by readers over time [Negroponte, 1995,
> p. 70]

The text and message has several embodiments, which are auto-
matically derived from the same data. For example, the reader
can interpret one stream of bits contained in a weather report in
many different ways, and the viewer can look at the same bits
from many different perspectives.

The digital world rests on quantum reality and physics,
which was the new version of science developed in the twentieth century. Classical physics of the previous centuries viewed
matter as being determined, localized, and causal. At the sub-
atomic level all matter is composed of waves and particles. They
are possessed of infinite possibilities. Every neurobiological,
elemental event is related to other elemental events and to the
cosmos at large through waves and particles. The Heisenberg
principle states that either the wave or the particle can be meas-
ured, but not both at the same time, because only a wave or a
particle exists for an observer at any one time. In a superim-
posed state, a wave of all the atoms that exist contains all that
has ever been thought and ever will be thought in the cosmos.
When a wave configures as a particle, it becomes a piece of
information, a fragment of knowledge, a shard of the infinite.
Waves and particles are immortal, invisible, and hidden from
our eyes.

Wilfred Bion proposed two forms of thought, which, he
readily admitted, were mythical constructs: alpha-type elements
and beta-type elements, as he called them. The former are suitable for dream storage and subsequent thinking, for they can be
appreciated by ordinary thought. If they are not capable of being
transformed by thinking, they remain as mentally indigestible
beta-type elements. As beta-elements, and quantum waves, they
remain part of a universe of strong emotions that cannot be used

for thinking. They constitute the unconscious and infinite that each human being contains and remain as a formidable obstacle to thinking, to making experience finite and known.

These beta-elements are the matrix from which thought has the potential to be realized, but they can remain trapped as raw, sensual facts that are incapable of being thought about. This is because they are things and have personality, and, as such, they can only remain as undigested and incapable of being transformed by the alpha-process. They come to sabotage the process of making finite what was the infinite, because they have a dreadfulness that cannot be named and thought about: they are too frightening and too difficult to contemplate. This dreadfulness goes some way towards explaining the tension between the finite and the infinite, the known and the unknown. The emotions aroused by the dreadfulness sabotage the process of thinking by not attaining the state of alpha-elements (Bion, 1963).

Simplifying Bion's explanation, it can be said that beta-elements are waves, but in configuring as particles, they become alpha-elements. Dream-work can be seen as a continuous wave function, but dreams and thought are particles.

All the discoveries of the twentieth century can be understood to have been wrested from the infinite. The evidence that that discoveries and inventions arise from dreams is overwhelming—for example, the invention of lead-shot by William Watts in the eighteenth century, and the invention of the first sewing-machine by Elias Howe. The Duke of Bridgewater had a problem in distributing coal. He gave the problem to an artisan, who went to bed for three days and dreamt of canals. The result was the beginning of the network of canals that crossed Britain in the eighteenth century, to bring coal and, subsequently other goods to the consumers.

From the time of Charles Babbage with his analytic machine through to Alan Turing's invention of the Turing Machine, the digital age was born. Text, sound, video, and numbers can now be put into digital form, to be stored and processes by computers.

In a sense, digital technology is an analogue of dream-work. How one works with a dream through free association—by being aware of synchronicity, by converting from image to word, by discerning the implicit order and seeing the meaning of the symbolism—is exactly how digital technology works. One hypothesis is that social dreaming could not have been re-discovered without the groundswell of quantum physics and digital technology.

Sándor Ferenczi was a contemporary of Freud and a pioneering psychoanalyst living in Hungary. One of Ferenczi's preoccupations was how mathematics came into existence: Does mathematics owe its existence to the universe or to the human psyche? Why does the universe follow the mathematical creation of the human mind?

One, seemingly outrageous, hypothesis can be that humans dreamt of it all in the first instance! The evidence comes from scientists themselves, such as Einstein, but also from the fact that Ernst Mach and Theodore Gomperz both published books on dreaming in the late nineteenth century, 20-odd years before Freud (Keve, 2000).

The working hypothesis of this chapter is the outcome of trying to understand the experience and phenomena of social dreaming, which is different from, but complementary to, therapeutic dreaming.

CHAPTER NINE

Working hypotheses on social dreaming

It would be rash and omnipotent to outline a theory of social dreaming. What can be offered is a series of working hypotheses that have been substantiated repeatedly since 1982. What, therefore, exists is an emergent theory.

1. It is possible to dream socially. This hypothesis, validated in 1982, when the first social dreaming matrix was held at the Tavistock Institute, has been reconfirmed time and time again.

2. Dreaming received in a matrix is different from dreaming received in a group, or in the situation of the psychothera-peutic couple. To whom one tells the dream is critical, for the dream changes to fit the context. This is because the mental space of a group is different from that of a matrix—not better or worse, but different. The mental space of a group tends to fill with finite knowledge as participants exercise their au-thority and leadership. By contrast, the matrix tends to fill with the infinite as it taps the web of unconscious emotions

and feelings among the participants. The idea of the not-known becomes more tenable. Matrix and group can be seen as complementary. In a matrix, the dreams are the currency; in a group, the relationships of the participant dreamers are the focus.

The dreams recounted in a matrix differ from other social contexts in that personal psychic factors are screened out by the dreamers. The dreams are social in that they are more firmly embedded in the environmental context of the dreamer.

3. This is because the matrix is a "container" for receiving the dreams that is different from any other. Consequently, the "contained" of the dream alters: the narrative content of the dream changes. The dreams recounted in this short book are of quite a different form from personal dreams as would be given in the therapeutic context.

4. The matrix alters the nature of thinking, which is derived more from the infinite than from finite consciousness. In a group, the concern is to create a universe of meaning to which everyone can subscribe. This universe is rationally and logically determined and proceeds by people convincing others by argument. Thought is what the group trades in. By contrast, in the matrix a "multi-verse" of meaning arises out of the dreams and the free associations, and a plethora of meanings can sit side by side. This is because the thinking in a matrix comes from the unknown, or what is not-known, and is derived from a no-thought. The thinking produced in a matrix just is. It comes from our emotions. This matrix thinking leads to new thoughts that have, in all probability, never been thought before. Thinking is what the matrix trades in, using the currency of dreams.

5. Social dreaming questions the notion that dreams are personal possessions, which they undoubtedly are in a therapeutic situation. The concern in social dreaming is with the socio-centric, with being in touch with the environment and aware of the totality of the systemic universe that is around

us. One value that emerges is that participants find themselves tolerant of what the matrix is exploring.

6.   Social dreaming can be used as a tool of research and consul-
     tancy—that is, action research. The evidence comes from
     work done in Australia, the United States, Britain, and Italy.

7.   This is the most disturbing hypothesis. The Spanish writer
     and philosopher Unamuno suggested that we are as humans
     "a dream, a dream that dreams" (1954). There is sufficient
     evidence to show that inventors and discoverers dream what
     they are puzzling about. Australian aborigines refer to the
     Dreamtime—an ancient time when the land, its features, its
     people, and its gods were dreamt into existence. If, however,
     we rely exclusively on our consciousness and do not take
     account of the unconscious, we are cutting ourselves off from
     our creativity.

8.   Dreaming enlarges the space of the possible for thinking. It is
     always inducting us to the tension between the conscious
     and the unconscious. the finite and the infinite, between
     knowing and not-knowing.

9.   The experience of a social dreaming matrix places partici-
     pants in the domain of searching for knowledge and insight
     as it makes use of scientific method: that is, working hypoth-
     eses. This places participants in the realm of Sphinx (knowl-
     edge) as opposed to that of Oedipus (the psyche of the
     person).

10. The hypothesis is that dreaming is a wave function and
     dreams and thoughts are particles, according to quantum
     physics.

11. One hypothesis that emerged quickly in the social dreaming
     matrix was that transference issues were focused not on the
     hosts, but on the dreams. It was found that if the transference
     issues were addressed directly in the matrix, the dream was
     robbed of the opportunity to explore these issues. To address
     them directly was to convert the matrix into the safe and
     known domain of group, and as a result the integrity of the

dreaming was compromised and denuded of its potential richness.

12. The dream matrix is a transitional object. It comes to be understood by all participants as a safe, shared space outside of the individual for the exploration of dreaming. The dreams are transformed from images into thinking in everyday, logical thoughts that are newly formed and so creative for the dream-participant. Because the matrix engages in this transformation of thinking and thought, the matrix has the potential for being a transitional object for all the participants. It is the experience of working in the ambience of dream thinking that allows individuals to make changes in their work and life. The evidence is that changes do occur for participants.

The experience of social dreaming is an end in itself in that thinking is transformed. It becomes a transitional object in which all can participate. Communication through dreaming creates a spontaneous, free way of relating to what has been lost in modern societies. These are some of the initial working hypotheses that we have found useful in the work of social dreaming.[1]

Is dreaming just junk?

Francis Crick—one of the discoverers of DNA—and Graeme Mitchison put forward the junk theory of dreams. They argued that during REM sleep, which is the evidence that dreaming is occurring during sleep, what is happening is that the brain's neocortex is bombarded by a series of bangs that emanate from the brainstem. These random bangs, Crick and Mitchison argue, shake lose the parasitic information that would otherwise clog up the brain. Therefore, dreams do not make sense and are junk to be discarded (Crick & Mitchison, 1983).

While they were able to identify the mechanism, they mistook its function. Another neurobiologist and mathematician, George Christos (2003), asks: why do we dream, and do our dreams mean anything? His concern is the creative human mind.

He recognizes that humans store an estimated hundred billion neurons of the brain as patterns of connectivity. Memories are represented as "attractors". This is when neurons are in the same state of quiescence. From this distributed storage of memory emerge properties that distinguish the brain from a computer—for example, a typing error will produce an erroneous response from a computer's memory, but a correct memory in the brain.

Input to the brain can result in an attractor, which is not itself a memory but is made up of components of existing memories. These are known as "spurious states". Christos argues that these spurious states are not junk but allow human beings to generate creative new ideas from their existing memories.

The function of this random brainstem stimulation is to unlearn, or put into question, the terrain of memory, with the result that creative solutions are more likely to be generated (Christos, 2003).

It is unknown as yet whether or not the brain can actually produce attractor nets. Nevertheless, Christos offers a fertile working hypothesis that does much to repair the damage done to the very idea of dreaming by Crick and Mitchison.

After this extended foray into the realm of working hypotheses, the following chapter gives more evidence on a social dreaming matrix and demonstrates the continual transformations of thinking that take place.

Note

1. These hypotheses, and others, are contained in books and articles—for example, Lawrence (1998a, 2003).

CHAPTER TEN

Case study

This matrix took place on 29 November 2003. It was for a group of 40 psychotherapists who had no experience of social dreaming but entered it in a spirit of exploration. The social dreaming session lasted from 10 to 11.30 a.m. and was followed by a session that had the primary task of "being available for thinking".

Dream 1

> (Preamble to Dream 1: I usually have "doing" dreams, so this dream is unusual.)

> *I am at home and get up and look out of the window of my house. I notice that some buildings, which are normally across the road, have disappeared. I feel shocked, and then I see all the buildings disappear, including trees and houses. I feel quite upset as well as feeling small and young.*

Dream 2

> *I am on top of Cable Mountain, looking down, not knowing whether I can get down. It feels dangerous, as I am not sure what is down there. I feel helpless and frightened.*

Association: The being frightened in the dream reminds me of a dream of terror:

Dream 3

> *There is an execution about to happen; there are some very dark-skinned people around. I had to get information across somewhere in order to save maybe a child being executed. In the end, though, a small black boy was executed. I felt the horror of it and felt as though I myself was twelve or thirteen.*

Association: Reminds me of a dream I had as a child:

Dream 4

> *I was going to be shot by my favourite uncle and woke up crying. Feelings of dismay, fear, and anxiety.*

Dream 5

> *I am at my old university campus and notice that the buildings around are so clear and the people are so clear, but despite this I am convinced that I will not get my degree.*

Dreamer adds, "Even though I did graduate."

Association: This reminds me of a complex dream that seems to have two parts:

Dream 6

> End part: *I am on an American University campus. I am in the residential area, where there are lots of areas of water, with swimming and competing. I am in discussion with a child, trying to work out who the parents are.*

Middle part: *I am at the residential part of the campus. There is a decorator in my room, and I have a feeling he is not doing what I want him to do. He is clearing things out. He is also complaining about the music being too loud. When I go in, though, I realize that he had done a great job, with a very beautiful blue ceiling: a sense of being open to the sky.*

Dream 7

A lucid dream—*I am looking out of the window—a cul de sac— I think to myself, I am awake, but maybe if I am not awake, I should be able to fly. I try this and fall splat onto the bed. I then start walking in the garden. There is a dead colleague lying on the grass. Hi! I have no feelings about this. I look out on the road, and it is called RUEAR.*

Association: I was thinking of Christmas festivities and a snowy white place, and I remembered this dream:

Dream 8

I was in Munich and was driving my car the wrong way around a roundabout. I got confused. "Which way was I supposed to drive, and where was I?"

Dream 9

I am in London, and I am at a roundabout and get confused about which way to go around, and then I find myself saying, "If you don't think, you'll know, but if you think, you won't."

Dream 10

I am static in water, floating on top of it. I can see water in every direction going on endlessly. There are colourful objects in the water, floating. I look down into the water and feel a bit anxious as I am also naked and feel exposed.

Dream 11

> *I am in my home town near the sea, and there are some huge waves rolling in. My thoughts grow as the waves grow and then going down slowly, like in slow motion. It is very gradual and has a sense of poetry.*

Associations: The wish to be the anti-thesis causes so much anxiety.

- "Dover Beach" by Matthew Arnold—a poem about sadness and anxiety.
- Waves going in and out . . . freedom . . . Lagos . . . pains of growing up.
- We are living in a world that we cannot predict any more. We struggle through the business of living—good bits and bad bits, all mixed in.
- Knowledge of the world of the here-and-now reminds me of a neighbour who was frightened of going to Brent Cross shopping centre because of terrorists, but got run over by a car.
- Dreams about this professional association . . . fears about communication . . . anxiety about finishing things and being successful; the heaviness of permanent things disappearing and the feeling of isolation.
- In the first dream I felt loss and grief . . . a sense of death, not fear. Not being able to feel fear.
- What is real, the material nature of life or the dream? RUEAR [Are you 'ere?]
- *Matrix* film was about a naïve reality. Maybe there is a question around psychotherapy training.

Dream 12

> A dream about *a single chair in a room.*

Associations: What furniture do you have left after training. Lost what you had, but what have you gained? 25 years. Solid things melt into the air. Can't imagine the object any more. What does it mean to say, this professional society in the past and in the future?

- Re-organization of profession . . . things being swept away . . . opening up the new vistas.

Dream 13

I have been elected to be the only woman member of Michael Howard's cabinet. I am walking with my face turned to the wall as I am being congratulated all the time by everybody.

Associations: Wailing Wall.

- Different pieces of furniture are necessary like different ideas, so you are seen and do not disappear.
- Ronnie Laing used to live around here: opposite the church on the corner outside this building.
- Impotence in this world. It is all too big—how guilty we are, how responsible we are. How do we manifest ourselves as individuals? As *this* individual. Furniture—be all and end all. Waves—relentlessness of them—their inability to stop. Waves are not personal. In spite of me, the waves happened.

Dream 14

I am at a hospital in Jerusalem, where I am going into the cancer ward. It is light and bright, and I can see the blue sky through the ceiling. I have an amazingly comfortable, cared-for feeling. There is no distress at all.

Associations: Waves and tides are governed by the moons. Even though we live in a sophisticated individual world, we are puny compared to the natural forces of the world.

- This reminds me that it is a whole year since I adopted my two children, and they have grown, and this is sad.
- Being grown up—25 years—you cannot pretend you do not know anything any more. I don't like being grown up . . . I

want to be silly. I am tired of having to drive the car all the time . . . a terrible strain . . . having to use one's ego all the time, whereas below these things there is a child at a Christmas market—where does that go?

– The child is like the social unconscious and operates with a different logic.

– Michael Howard is an older, grown-up leader of the opposition, unlike the children before him. The cancer-ward dream makes me think of moving away from something we know to the opposite stance. The unknowing is in the middle. Speaking of children, my son was 3 months old when I was doing my training, and now he is 17. When he was young, he was lovely, and I enjoyed nurturing him, but now he is out of control and does not like me very much.

– I was thinking of the anti-war marches and remembered the following dream:

Dream 15

I am on the march with my grandchildren, and Jo, my youngest, needs to have a pee. I feel somewhat irked that he had that drink against my advice, but I take him. When we come back, everybody has disappeared, and everything seems rather barren. We are wandering around but cannot find anybody. Jo takes my hand, and we go around and round, and it occurs to me that maybe he knows something that I do not.

Associations: Youth, and ideas, and hope. All that we have, we can keep that intact, at least. Hold on to values. The consistency of the ebb and flow of water. Not the danger. The consistency of this professional society hanging on to that while we have our fears and fantasies. I don't know what this society is or what it was. Discovering faith in the grandson . . . knowing and not knowing. Sad, but also comforting about growing into an unknowing being. Watery dreams don't overwhelm me. The cancer-ward dream was about going into a new experience. It was a good feeling.

- I recently found myself being dismissed by insurance companies, as though being caught up in a dream and then reality. I still have my work and responsibility and am faced with what counts and what does not. Knowing and not knowing. Change and old age are about developing.

Dream 16

I was driving, and every hundred yard there would be a traffic light, and I came to a roundabout where there were 15 traffic lights. I felt overwhelmed by this knowing world.

Associations: When the Shah fell in the Iranian revolution of 1978, the first thing that people did was to drive up one-way streets the wrong way.

- I remember having a dream when I was ending my therapy:

Dream 17

In the dream I was leaping into water, and I remember there were traffic lights: red, green, and amber, and red meant stop, and green meant go.

I stopped my therapy so that I could move on—that is, go.

Associations: Life ... death ... loss and knowledge of death. We are on a journey, and the question is how we find a path. How to live. I am aware that our professional society is about to lose its building, which I have got used to. Ants live in rented houses. There is only one traffic light in the Orkneys, where there is also no need for psychotherapists.

- Free association gives up absolute meaning and opens things up to a multi-verse of meanings. When there is emptiness in front of you, you can take something different and rebel against traffic lights and order and control rather than face an unknowing giving up. Being in the sea reminds me of this society in the sea, with all these new rules from the dreaded UKCP (United Kingdom Council of Psychotherapy) rather than letting us be free to work. This society was founded as a place against the establishment . . . look at you now!

– This reminds me of *Les Miserables*: a song I cannot get rid of in my mind at the moment . . . "I dreamed a dream of time gone by when hope was high and life worth living . . ." Also, there is a part where they shout "Clear away the barricades!"—a feeling of optimism. But also the dream song has another part: "now life has killed the dream I dreamed".

– Castaneda's . . . pick up a rabbit and kill it. It is your time. The maternal dying, but the other isn't horrendous. Cancer is horrific. It is another dying, and inevitable, and we don't understand it. Dreaming alerts us to this. "Sleep is death stirred by dreams, and death is dreamless sleep."

– Ronny Laing had a stuffed rhino, and we still have it. Chaotic, and can go off the rails. It is in our logo. Isn't the rhino an endangered species? A tough, thick-skinned creature that is very dangerous and endangered. Going against the traffic is both of these. Swimming against the tide. Going up streets the wrong way.

– I sometimes find that when I am stressed, I am comforted by my patients, and I get as much out of my consulting-room as my patients. Maybe I am going down a familiar way. Lacan spoke of there being no truth. A world without rules. The only rule is to take the dream seriously. Listening very important . . . Are you 'ere? This reminds me of the container again: Lacan . . . another way of being.

Dream 18

> *I am in a room, and there are two mothers with two spoons which are standing up. I noticed a wooden chair in the room as the only furniture.*

Associations: The two mothers are Sue and Veronica, with two implements to feed you with or not feed you with. Reminds me of a time when I had Jimmy Witherspoon playing, and when someone shouted "Bring up spoon!" a child in the audience felt that this was very funny. I took the most money I have ever taken from a gig that night, and with that money I was able to buy a house in Lyme Regis.

- Two mothers . . . not here today . . . vision. Tension between two mothers, a discord. Reminds me of *détente*—the loss of the bipolar world means we live in more dangerous times. Did you say *des tantes*—the aunts—two words?

- What about fathers . . . fathers who collapsed. This reminds me of Ecclesiastes: "A time to rejoice, a time to cry, time for change." Veronica is not here today because she is at her grandchild's first birthday. Being with my children . . . careers and priorities. Bernie is also another father. The dream of the baby whose parentage is uncertain. The baby is, it seems, a boy. Maybe it is about a group of people being around. Bernie/Sue/Veronica . . . father and mother. There are new people—a circle of people—a new parentage?

- Reminds me of a painting by Leonardo da Vinci of two mothers with a baby, where the mothers looking in different directions. Reminds me of roundabouts and also the roads in India, where it looks like chaos but there are very few accidents. It is amazing how few accidents can happen when people look in different directions.

- *Détente* . . . reminds me of tents that are folded, moved, and fragile. The traffic lights remind me of UKCP and structures, and Kevin the old Chair, and how he disappeared, and a new group emerged. Spirit . . . change . . . death . . . renewal. Reminds me of my garden. We are now in the autumn and winter, and things have died, but there will be renewal in the spring, and regeneration. The rhythmic feel to nature is comforting. But there is a fear and the shock of moving again. Isledon Road [the house of the society] had stability. Reminds me of the dream of the houses disappearing. Being homeless, and the importance of stability and values.

- The founders are disappearing, and it can be a relief when the founders go. New founders needed to unfold the tent. Tents remind me of nomads. Houses not necessary, but tents express a need for fluidity . . . essence. People's time comes and goes.

– I remember Tom Ormay [a Hungarian group analyst] when I was training. He told a story once of being in a café watching a mother with her baby. The mother kept pulling the baby's face to look at her, and this really disturbed Tom. Maybe that is part of the essence: look away, and never look back.

– It is static and dangerous to never be able to look away. This reminds me of when I was told to move into the circle at the beginning of today's session when I was not ready for it. What is going on outside, in the profession? Feel we are being dragged, kicking and screaming. Nomads shifting. "No-mad professional society"—joined not to be mad. There is creativity in being mad. Those of us who joined were in some ways nomads. The great strength in being a nomad is the ability to move on. How do we do that? All sorts of things can give us structure. Be separate. Détente . . . aunts . . . nomads.

– It was a mad struggle to get people to come to this event today. What is that about? What is it that we do? Nomads are able to wonder around like members. But nomads also need charismatic leaders. Freedom comes from strong leadership. There is an unspoken assumption here, as nomads cannot do as they please. They have a prescribed path in order to survive, following water and food. They are generally a group like us and don't necessarily need a leader. They may have a strong sense of leadership, even though they may deny it, and this is necessary to remain a nomadic tribe.

– The chaos of trying to get people back home for Christmas is a bit like getting people here. Nomadic leaders are necessary for practical and spiritual tasks. The two things need to link. Nomadic tribes have a historical structure and culture they follow. We have a structure and history. Nomads had to learn from their environment. Reminds me of camels—cigarettes. It's the tobacco that counts! It's the player that counts!

* * *

The matrix ended and was followed by a "Thinking Session", which lasted from 11.50 a.m. until 12.40 p.m.

This opened with a statement of the purpose of the session as being available for thinking.

This started from the four kinds of thinking expressed in chapter three. There are four ways of thinking: thinking as being and thinking as becoming—these are more or less conscious; by contrast, thinking as the unthought known and thinking as dreaming are unconscious. The first two are set in the light of consciousness, so to speak, and the second set is in the shadow. We need both kinds of thinking.

Discussion and associations

- The theme of disappearing houses. Not fear of desolation, but facing the reality of desolation.
- The sadness of the past in the professional association and founders. Hope for the future—the little boy peeing—being.
- A history that has not been told. The dark secrets and the dread of putting things together.
- Remember as a child, my father throwing me into the waves as a baby and catching me . . . a sense of strength and structure through taking a risk.
- A buoy is something that floats.
- Penis . . . getting rid of waste material.
- Infancy means one also has to grow up into adulthood.
- Thing get thrown up into the air. How do they come down?
- Being caught.
- Buoyancy, knowing when one arrives at the end of therapy.
- We are being carried by a stage in our society.
- A stage has not been reached yet.
- Being lost and being found.
- Trust in leaders and authority.

- Trusting ourselves together as an organization.
- Can I throw a spanner in this discussion? We are fastening onto our professional society because we are here, but it feels a bit thin. Maybe we are avoiding issues to do with mortality and immortality—growing old and growing up—these are grave matters.
- What does the continuity of our society actually represent?
- Maybe we are having this conversation at this time of year due to seasons. Mortality, things dying at this time of year . . . Christmas . . . birth and life of Christ. He was born and then he died, and what about his wilderness years? What about our society's wilderness years? From grandchild to child. Nice to be put into context.
- I am another generation down, looking in different directions.
- This is a bit like Kleinian therapy, where everything comes back to the origin.
- Important to be a new generation.
- Strange and mournful: Am I joining a dying organization?
- Peeing is a release. Picking sweet peas in my garden.
- Trying to produce seeds.
- Flower dies, but something else emerges.
- Spanner? A grave issue to do with death and dying.
- People are not here.
- Maybe we need this focus as a metaphor in a world of chaos.
- The black boy having his head cut off.
- The outside world impinges on our current lives.
- Peeing . . . PING!
- Waking up to another layer or reality.
- The overlap between inside and outside.
- The mood is low and heavy.
- The overlap is with another space—the unthought known.
- It is not about pessimism, but it can be a scary place.

- All religions have been preoccupied with the tension between the timeless spirit/mind and the limited body. How does one live with such a tension. Jesus on the cross is a metaphor for this suffering place.
- Spirit and matter in our society.
- In social dreaming you are at the edge of infinite space, and this is exciting.
- Can we know the unconscious? We are always leaving and always coming. There is change all the time. Pain all the time . . . differences. Waves . . . coming and going. Waves can be very choppy.
- Amazed we are going through this process.
- Who are the members? Feel like we are in the ocean . . . where is the membership?
- Need to hear and share about our members.
- Hang on, there is a world and a profession out there, and things are changing outside, which will affect us out there— not inside.
- We are a third-generation organization.
  First generation: strong and motivated.
  Second generation: reactive.
  Third generation: loses the plot.
- We are together because we are supposed to be together.
- The internal drivers are very weak.
- In 2008 the UKCP is planning that we all become individual members rather than membership through our training organization. This may be a huge opportunity.
- The perennial drama is between the narcissistic and the socialistic way of being, and the need is for the two to collaborate.
- Religion and faith in our society.
- I felt abandoned by the society, but now I feel more involved.
- Faith in world means we can go on living.
- Spirit of the organization is being represented by the trust

that people have in bringing their dreams. This means that we are communicating and are on a level, like the floating water with all the bits. What connection do we have with each other? Is the furniture internal, or external, or both? We are the missing bits of a good number of members.

– I don't feel that the body is dying. The trainees are the future. This is a sort of re-union, as I don't feel so stuck in my year as you tend to.

– Creativity gets lost, things become reactive, members feel impinged upon. An idea has been mooted that trainees should become full members from the beginning. This will enthuse the membership and has been discussed at UKCP level. I think it is a good idea, but it is not popular with us.

– Can member organizations transform? We need to get away from the imperialism of the universities. There is no union for psychotherapists to develop the profession. This could be an exciting development. We and the UKCP, though, are looked down on by the BAP [British Association of Psychotherapists] aristocracy. The UKCP are the peasants. Why cannot we communicate?

– We are the outsider organization where all the vagabonds come to who could not get in anywhere else. Maybe you should look at who you are and have an identity rather than being a bunch of rogues.

– We have got it as well as it can be. There is always room for improvement, and this is something worth waiting for. Variety is valuable, and the newcomers vs. the retirees gives the organization a dialectical feel.

– Do we recognize our elders? Quite worried about that! We had a very good report from an assessment board recently.

– Why do people join us? Because we are different from the establishment, like the BAP.

– Faith . . . pee . . . emotions. Faith is the container. We have the container and need to concentrate on changing the content where a whole new world can open up.

- I have a dream of different modalities of psychotherapy living with each other.
- Dream on!

Discussion

Here, in this case study, we can see the flow of dreaming and thinking as these occur. The evidence is that people are thinking all the time, but normally they keep quiet about it. The participants are learning to pass between their private inner world of thinking and the public domain of other people. In a matrix there are no difficulties as to what is to be assimilated. There are no apparent conventions of duplicity being followed.

The SDM allows people to learn that what they would regard as private can be made public. The result for many participants is that because their thought processes have been agitated, they find themselves able to think—in their work situation, for example—in innovative ways, able to look at their problems from different angles.

Systemically, the SDM seems to be about professional growth through training and education. It also raises questions for each participant about the losses and gains of understanding that come through examining lived experiences. From the very first dream of disappearing buildings and the bird's eye view of the dreams immediately following, there is a sense of taking stock of what was regarded as known and the unknown. The finite ↔ infinite are very much present. "Are you here" in the dreams is one question.

This is linked to the dreams and associations about training and about the characters—dead and alive—involved, much later in the matrix. There is the questioning of what their professional society means (part of the furniture), which is linked to the proposed major reorganizations of the UKCP and the BAP.

Running through the matrix is the appreciation of younger colleagues and the very young, children and grandchildren, which represent hope for the future. At the same time, because of the first dreams describing terrors, execution, shooting by an uncle, they are alluding to something dreadful that has happened in the history of the organization that has not been repaired; but probably few of the participants are aware of this in conscious memory.

Roundabouts and traffic lights feature as indications of how people are finding their way through the existential maze of their profession. Tragedy, for example, represented by the cancer ward, is recognized, as well as the positive aspects of living.

The meaning for participants of matrix and free association are explored, as is creativity. There is recognition of the matrix through the film of the same name, and free association is seen as liberating.

The free associations have been reported in full to give the full flavour of the SDM. Readers have an opportunity to develop their own working hypotheses.

CHAPTER ELEVEN

Social dreaming
as the shadow of the future

We live in a multidimensional universe. This is the astounding fact that has emerged from contemporary cosmology. We live in parallel universes. Time can go backwards as well as forwards. The universe is queerer than we think, even suppose. The implications of these, and other cosmological facts, are not our subject, but social dreaming is.

Dreams occur when there is a juxtaposition of a disturbed environment, such as political unrest, or the contemporary *milieu* of terrorism and uncertainty, and a disturbed inner terrain of memory in the unconscious. The disturbed terrain of memory coincides with the timelessness of the unconscious. Emotions are aroused that will trigger the dreaming. Consequently, we dream in the *now* forgotten memories of the *past* of humanity. These appear to be "shadows of the future cast before" (Bion, 1994). In actuality, they are the outcome of the resonance between the contemporary environment and memory traces in the unconscious. Nevertheless, they alert us to what is being unconsciously thought in the environment.

The September 11th hijackers—and all terrorists—use our own deepest dreams of self-destruction against ourselves. The evidence is that perpetrators of September 11 had access to PC versions of flight simulation. These are the product of dreaming as thinking. When bin Laden planned his attack, he did not count on his followers and their wives starting to dream of the destruction of America. He became so worried that he told one supporter not to tell his dream to others, otherwise the secret would be out.

The September attack was being foreshadowed in dreams throughout the world. This is not to be wise after the event, but to recognize that people will repeat in their dreams the horrors that have befallen humanity in the past. To repeat: these "memory traces can also be considered as a shadow the future casts before" (Bion, 1994).

Mind and body (and matter) share quantum reality, which underlies *both* the brain as a physical object *and* the mental events of consciousness. This comes about in the way that the cortex and the nervous system interact, which has only been discovered in the last century. Quantum physics explains in a startling way both the behaviour of matter and energy and the mental world of the mind. Reality is not just out there in the environment, but inside every human being. Quantum physics is an explication of the implicit "stuff" that rests within all the explicit objects that make up our environment. Quantum reality is based on the behaviour of waves and particles; it takes explanations far beyond the causes and effects of traditional physical science and opens up synchronicity and more indeterminate linkages between events. Quantum physics gives us a clearer picture of what constitutes reality both outside and inside human beings.

The basic fact of reality is that it is composed of waves, which are spread-out flappy kinds of things, and particles, which are bullet-like entities. Both consciousness and the unconscious rely on these to have existence and to think.

One hypothesis can be that the whole world not only goes about its conscious business of living but has also a parallel universe of dreaming in its unconscious world. This might be called a "dreamscape". Furthermore, the whole world might be linked through the wave functions of the dreamscape, which operates as a matrix of the social unconscious.

In the mid-1990s in a social dreaming matrix at the William Alanson White Institute in New York, one dreamer offered a dream in which *he was trapped on a high floor of the Twin Towers; it was after an aeroplane had crashed into it.* At the time, the dream registered, but there were no residues of previous experience that could be noted, and the event was unimaginable for the other participants in the matrix.

The alleged planner of the Twin Towers catastrophe has been identified as Osama bin Laden. In a tape of a conversation with his colleagues, which was recorded in Afghanistan and published by The Associated Press in December 2002, his colleagues talk over food about the beneficence of Allah in making things possible. They refer to various mosques, complimenting the clerics on their sermons. They rejoice in how they are being heard throughout the Muslim world and how, as a result, young men are being attracted to their cause. In a series of simplistic arguments they all argue that Allah will be triumphant. They live in a split world: they are good, and the enemies of Allah are bad. One gets a glimpse of how the Crusaders might have talked in earlier centuries.

One is struck by Hannah Arendt's observation on the "banality of evil" in this context. They are all doing simple things, like eating and having a conversation. They are blind to any consideration of the victims and their relatives. They are blind as they justify their actions. One is reminded of all the other instances of man's inhumanity to mankind. Conscience is put into abeyance, and guilt cannot be acknowledged.

Bin Laden is congratulated on the results of the September attack. The pride of the engineer comes out as he describes how the steel supporting the Twin Towers building would melt. They are all triumphant.

There is talk of visions and dreams, as if the evidence of dream would support their millenarian cause. One young man reports that he had a dream. "I saw it in a dream. *We were playing a soccer game against the Americans. When our team showed up on the field, they were all pilots. So I wondered if it was a soccer game or a pilot game. Our players were pilots.*" The young man knew nothing of the operation until he heard it on the radio. Bin Laden said that this was a good omen. Someone else claims to have had a vision of an aeroplane crashing into a tall building. He also knew nothing of the planned operation. Another, referring to dreams and visions, says that the aeroplane crashing into a building had been dreamt before by more than one person. He told of the wife of one of their followers, who had dreamt of the aeroplane crashing into a tall building the week before it happened.

Bin Laden reports that he was at a camp in Kandahar when one of the brothers came to him and said that he saw in a dream an *aeroplane crashing into a tall building in America*. In the same dream, he saw that *they were being taught karate.* "*At that point I was worried*", says Bin Laden "*that maybe the secret would be revealed if everyone starts seeing it in their dream. So I closed the subject. I told him that if he has another dream, not to tell anybody, because people will be upset with him.*" And would forewarn the victims, presumably.

The Al Qaeda master plan was in danger of becoming common knowledge through dreaming. The wave functions of dreaming became available to more and more people, for it could not be rationally controlled. The relationship between the actual events of destruction and the dream thoughts that fuel the resultant action become more apparent.

One explanation of this phenomenon is through the "transactional interpretation", which is a working hypothesis offered by Fred Wolf (1994). Using quantum physics, whereby dreams and thinking are composed of waves that coalesce as particles on occasion, Wolf (1994) argues that a quantum system exists in a superposition of states. Before they are observed, these all exist simultaneously. They become a single state once they are observed, because the act of observation, whether on a magnetic tape or in a computer memory, results in a "reduction of the wave packet". This takes place in a non-physical manner, and there is no explanation for it in physical–mathematical terms.

These waves are composed of "real" and "imaginary" parts: the former are represented by complex-number functions, the latter are subjective and exist only in the imagination. Working on the assumption, however, that these waves are objective and exist in the environment, it follows that they exist in time and space.

It is possible to compute the probability that a particular event will occur in real time and space by multiplying one wave by another wave. These waves are called "stimulating" and "responding" events. Whereas one wave moves forward in time, the other wave moves backward through time. The wave function of one dream will bring about the wave functions of other dreams. As Wolf explains this phenomenon:

> This idea that one multiplies two counterstreaming waves together, one coming from the present and one coming from the future, is called the transactional interpretation. What is new here is the idea that events, even those that haven't yet occurred, can generate these waves. [Wolf, 1994, p. 162]

This sounds absolutely bizarre, but it goes some way towards disentangling the relationship between dreaming and real events.

A dreamer has a dream of an actual event in the future. This dream of a planned event will create other dreams in other people who are in some way related to the original dreamer. This stimulating dream sparks responding dreams in others, because everyone is related in an unconscious matrix. The waves produced by these dreams, moving forward and backward in time, will coincide. If the resonance between these dreams as wave functions is weak, the chances of an actual event occurring will be that much more diminished. If, on the other hand, it is strong, the chances of an actual event occurring will be greatly enhanced (Figure 4).

The shadows of the future, it can be postulated, can be memories, dreams, and thoughts that are just floating around in

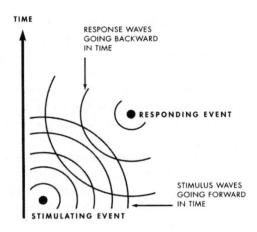

FIGURE 4:   Resonance between dream wave functions
(Wolf, 1994, p. 163).

the social unconscious that belongs to all. Some will be picked up and will initiate a responding event. Again, many of these will be deployed in the social unconscious, although they may be lodged in consciousness. When there is a strong association of stimulating and responding events, the chances of an actual event occurring in time and space will be heightened and actually take place in real time. Dream will lead to an act of destruction, but, equally, it can lead to creativity.

An example of the shadows of the future is found in a matrix in Israel. The theme of the matrix had been of houses and floors, symbolizing life and the fact of death. Three hours after this session, the marble floor of a wedding hall collapsed in Jerusalem, with the result that 31 guests were killed. Mira Erlich-Ginor (2003) was the host of this matrix, which continued for a number of weeks.

At the next matrix after the collapse, the participants asked themselves, did they foreshadow the future? It was uncanny. They concluded that they had been exploring through dreams the collapsibility of floors. One participant volunteered: "I read once that past and future, like here and there, are all at once. We dreamt before, but maybe the 'before' is the same time?"

The idea that the matrix had voiced the fragility of society and the collapsing floor was an example. The synchronicity discovered in the dreams mirrored the larger processes of society. There was a resonance between the social disturbances of the society and the actual dream of the collapsing floor.

One way of regarding consciousness in relation to the unconscious is to imagine the world as not only natural and physical, but also as a psychic pond. This is the matrix of the mind through which everyone is connected. As the philosopher Alfred North Whitehead said, the universe is pure mind. Thinking and thoughts can be likened to pebbles thrown into the psychic pond, setting off waves radiating from them. When two or more sets of these waves of thinking coincide, going forward and backward in time, an event is likely to occur. The phrase "shadows of the future cast before" takes on a new meaning. The shadows—subjective memories and dreams, cast before and backward (for time is relative)—bring about events and happenings that exist in real time and are objective. This is an example of reality being both "out there" and "in here"—both subjective and consensually agreed objectivity. (Objectivity is the clarification of one's own subjectivity in relation to others.) Dream has an important place in determining what takes place in day-to-day life.

To return to the discussion of quantum reality: as human beings, we need to put pictures to the equations once we go beyond the everyday world. Einstein was such a person. Famously, he talked of *Alte* [God] not playing dice, and he could not accept that there was another layer of reality below quantum reality waiting to be discovered. He could not accept on spiritual grounds, rather than physical, that there was indeterminacy in the Universe. In a 1935 paper he proposed a thought experiment concerning two electrons obeying quantum theory. He concluded that *no reasonable definition of reality* could be expected to permit the two electrons to be in interaction. Three decades ago, Einstein was proven wrong experimentally, without any shadow of doubt. The two electrons, no matter their distance apart, do relate to each other (Keve, 2004).

If dreams are accepted as subjective reality and dreaming and thinking are based on quantum reality, it could be that government intelligence services might initiate social dreaming matrices of their agents and their respondents, to check on what is being rationally and logically collected in the field. This would provide another way of triangulating from a different perspective the data being collected, which, at present, seems to be a best guess and is never perfect—to take Saddam's weapons of mass destruction as a case in point. Subjectivity would be tested against what is commonly agreed to be objectivity, which is consensual subjectivity in reality.

CHAPTER TWELVE

Conclusion

There have a number of applications of social dreaming. These are reviewed in appendix 2, where some of the experiments with social dreaming are outlined. Reviewing the evidence for social dreaming, which is the twenty-first-century, digital-age way of working with dreams, it can be seen that it is pivotal for thinking. Dreaming, which arises from our unconscious minds, is the origin of all our human thinking and thought. This, for the most part, is denied, for we continue to believe that all thought is initiated by the individual who operates in a thinking-free environment. It may well be that the human matrix, which is the root of all relationships and has existed among humans since their very beginnings, is composed of thoughts in search of a thinker, to echo Wilfred Bion. Mind is the apparatus that humans have evolved to pick up and transform these thoughts. In the same way, it can be suggested that there are dreams in search of a dreamer, but their reception depends on the extent to which the apparatus of mind can register and process both conscious and unconscious thinking.

Throughout this monograph it has been emphasized that a different vertex, or perspective, on dreaming has been taken. Knowledge is the concern, not the relationships, of the dreamer. It is the implicit knowledge of the dream, evoked by free association and amplification, that gives social dreaming its strength and richness of thinking.

Furthermore, social dreaming, it is being recognized, is a democratic venture, for the dream is what is important, not the status of the dreamer. Social dreaming puts us in touch with our unconscious and our thinking. And the unconscious is the roots of our human creativity. The infinite, in social dreaming, becomes less intractable and more available for transformation into finite knowledge.

It is also argued that social dreaming be adopted as part of the repertoire of action-researchers. Recent work in an international company, which is identifying the managerial structures for the containment of workers who are enormously stressed, could well initiate social dreaming. Some of the stress is caused by the fact that because of the time difference, some people have to work at night as they have to have email contact with the head office in Japan. The evidence is that the unconscious is structuring the conscious responses to employees' work. In addition to the interviewing, which has been the source of data, a SDM would give a vivid insight into how employees are emotionally involved in the life and work of the company by identifying their concerns and anxieties through their dreams. It can by hypothesized that the emotional quality of life at work will result in dreams, which will illumine symbolically the nature of the stress, anxiety, and feelings about the organization held in the mind so that they can be explored and thought about. Since the dream by its unconscious nature embodies the truth, the chances of finding a resolution to the company's problems are that much more enhanced.

A recent case study in Germany illustrates this (Lawrence, 2000a). The action-researchers recognized that the difficult organizational problems (a reorganization by the founder of the company) would be linked to the emotions, phantasies, and dreams of the members. They were all ambivalent about the change, ridden by doubts and anxieties, causing them to experience emotional pain and anguish.

As the action-researchers describe it, there was a forbidding atmosphere in the room, but with the recounting of one dream by Frau Z, this changed completely. Frau Z reported that she had not slept well for three nights. Finally she had a dream, which, she felt, was of some significance:

> She was in her bedroom at home, but it was not her home. It was a huge old mansion, spooky, dark, and cold. People came (adolescents perhaps). They tried to get to her, to get into the room, wanted to do something with her . . . something sexual, she thought. She fled in her night-gown into the street, but the people followed after her. She ran through the streets, the others in pursuit. . . . she awoke cold with sweat and full of anxiety.

The disclosure shocked the members, and they voiced their terrible anxieties about the reorganization, which they had felt unable to share with anyone. All had feelings of being pursued and of subtly being persuaded to do something against their will.

On the basis of this dream and other evidence, including the action-researchers' transference and countertransference feelings, they gave a working hypothesis that members were being asked to join a harem. Clearly, Frau Z's dream unlocked much of what could not be spoken of, and the dream became a pivotal event in the consultation and cut through all the rational explanations of why they were all finding it difficult to cooperate on the planned reorganization. They started to transform their thinking of events and came to a solution that satisfied everyone.

Social dreaming is a method for transforming thinking. That these transformations are not predictable makes social dreaming an adventure of the mind.

To conclude: dreaming, as one American writer put it, has a central role in our evolution, for:

> We must dream well if we are to confront forces threatening to annihilate us, and if we are to further the wonderful,

dangerous, and always visionary human adventure. [Lifton, 1987, p. 194]

On the basis of the evidence cited, can human beings afford not to dream socially to realize their innermost—and often unspoken—needs that are integral to the visionary human adventure?

The last word

The last word is given by Dr Colin James, a distinguished psychoanalyst and group analyst, who in 1974, in a chapter for an unpublished Festschrift for the writer, wrote the following:

Once I had read the brochure of the first Social Dreaming Conference, I was seized with the ideas of the "politics of revelation' in contrast to the 'politics of salvation' [Lawrence, 1994]. Wild horses would not have kept me from that event. A loud chord had been struck inside me.

Through the experience of the Social Dreaming Matrix, I became even more aware of factors in society which influenced me more than I had dared imagine previously.

I am familiar with the use of dreams in groups and of their value, including illuminating precisely relationships and attitudes in the life of a group with all its vicissitudes.

My experience in the Social Dreaming Matrix was, however, fundamentally different.

While this experience in no way took my personal approach to dreams away, something else was added. To begin with, the group dynamics of a gathering of thirty was for most of the time ignored, or at least noticed but not worked with. There were a few border skirmishes, but these did not seem to alter the direction of the event.

There was an initial tendency to look for group tensions and inter-group dynamics. The "dream" was made a central focus of attention. The social sharing of the dream was made a priority. Try as the participants might to force the consultants into transference objects, the consultants resisted any such attempt and focused on the dreams and their interconnectedness.

The dreams spanned the personal; the here-and-now; the world situation from many parts; the specific cultural struggle of people from across the world; political issues both local, national and international; the history of the world; of its anthropology; literature; poetry; myth from many cultures . . . to name but a few.

There was a growing sense of commitment to the task as people used the setting more confidently. Throughout the event there seemed to be a lessening of tension and anxiety about being wrong!

The staff were seen less as authority figures and more as facilitators. There remained the central axiom that we were intent to make ourselves available for dreams.

What was central was the forging of links between the dreams. The result was the possibility of new insights, new views and different senses of connectedness between people present in the matrix and back at base.

A sense of the "emergent" developed increasingly, interrupted by phases of disappointment and frustration . . .

Social Dreaming has helped me in my living in the world and for that I will remain grateful.

Gordon Lawrence's tenacity is well known and whilst he has kept diligently to the truth that he has discovered it has inevitably given rise to much conflict in his professional life. Nevertheless, the salient features of his credo, that of truth and commitment, integrity and resolve to portray faithfully that which experience has taught, results in our having to look more carefully at the features that influence us in our daily life.

The gist of the task of understanding the phenomenon of social dreaming, is to differentiate and yet integrate those forces within us which influence our behaviour and thinking and understanding with those forces from outside of us which impinge and influence our minds for good or bad. What influences the dreaming process? What is projected onto the dream of our personal life, and what from the social scene? What of each do we inhabit in our understanding?

APPENDIX 1

How does a social dreaming matrix work?

What the discovery of the social dreaming matrix necessitated was a re-thinking of the nature of dreaming, questioning the received knowledge, and inventing a method for capturing dreams in a setting that is quite different from the accepted two-person therapeutic method that has held sway since the beginning of the twentieth century. The method is outlined below.

1. The potential participants agree to take part in a SDM. Very often, it is appropriate to send out a simple brochure to the participants beforehand, stating the task of the SDM and the times of the meetings of the matrix.

2. In preparation for the meeting of the SDM, the chairs are arranged in a crude snowflake pattern, as shown in Figure 5. This arrangement facilitates the work of the SDM, for it breaks the pattern of a group, of chairs either in a circle or around a table. (In the figure, the block of four squares on the left represents chairs and is the basic building block of a matrix, which is represented on the right of the drawing.)

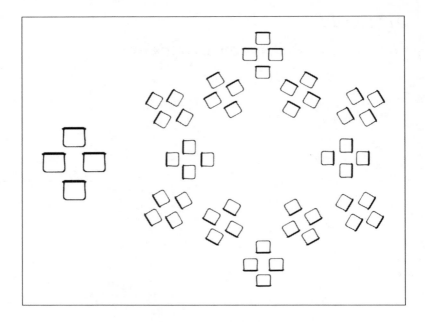

FIGURE 5:   Chair arrangement for an SDM.

By dividing the number of participants and the hosts—or takers—by multiples of four, the pattern of chairs can be arrived at. All the chairs face towards the centre of the room. This helps to create a freer thinking enclosure by breaking-up the usual configuration of the conventional group setting and not having the participants face each other.

3.   At the appointed time, the participants arrive, and each occupies a chair. The hosts, or takers, each also take a chair also. It is best if they distribute themselves around the matrix and do not sit together.

4.   One of the hosts welcomes the members and opens the SDM by stating the primary task.

5.   It will be found that a participant will offer a dream. It may be followed immediately with another dream, or it may be followed by a free association by one of the participants.

6. The host should never interpret individual dreams but, rather, be listening to the narrative and teasing out how the dreams may relate. The host is listening to the dream-content (the narrative) and trying to discern the dream-thoughts that are embedded in the story. (Guidance is offered throughout this text.) The host will be formulating and playing in their minds with working hypotheses based on the dreams.

   Nevertheless, it is often the case that people's responses to the dreams may be a form of interpretation in that they try to make sense of an image or narrative. However, rather than an ultimate truth, this will rarely be a finite statement but merely one idea that leads to many others.

7. In the unlikely event that a participant starts to interpret, directing attention to the dreamer and not holding to the dream and thus avoiding the work of the SDM, the host has to find a way of enabling the participants to get back to the task of the SDM by making some working hypothesis on the potential of the matrix.

8. Participants learn, however, how to pursue the task of the matrix. One must have experience to generate faith, or trust, in the dreaming process and the matrix, which will be unfolding before everyone.

9. When participants realize that there are no experts in social dreaming, they find the authority to play with their dreams, finding that free association is liberating. They also learn to tolerate not-knowing.

10. The role of the host is to be concentrating on the narratives of the dreams, associating to the dreams, finding out whether there are links between them, and making connections. The host then suggests a working hypothesis on what has been discovered.

11. This way of behaving in the matrix acts as a guide to the participants, though as they discover their own way of conducting themselves they give meaning to the matrix and become more totally involved in the richness of the dreams and the process of the matrix. In this way, participants in the

SDM quickly manage themselves in their roles as dreamers in the matrix and as people committed to understanding the dream.

12. The taking up of the role of dreamer in the matrix-as-a-system is a paradox. Compared to all the other rational roles one takes up in systems, in the matrix one is not taking up the same role but is standing outside it, being free to associate without hindrance and to think, sometimes bizarrely, without monitoring the thought processes. It is a kind of reversed role, but nevertheless a role in the matrix-as-system.

However, some intensive participation in a social dreaming matrix is an essential initial experience for those who would understand the matrix before setting one up.

APPENDIX 2
Applications of social dreaming

The evidence for the use of social dreaming in organizational systems comes from a young colleague, among others, who is an organizational consultant. He writes in a personal communication of 2003:

> About the efficacy of dreams in organizations, listen to this story. I had just completed a year-and-a-half consultation with the social services department of a major hospital. During this period, besides the regular work with the management, there were eight day-long meetings with the entire staff of about 40 people. Five of these working days included 2 dreaming sessions (social dreaming matrix) each. By the 6th session, I chose not to continue with the dreaming.
>
> The heart of the story lies in the feedback given to me at the end of the consultation, which was judged by all to be successful. A number of people cited the dreaming as the most important part of the work. It was seen as fresh, unique, and enriching. The negative feedback that I received had to do with my decision to stop the dreaming. *I was attacked for*

not carrying through with it [italics added]. I was never so happy to receive criticism!

In a different hospital, I worked with the senior nursing staff using dreams to address organizational issues. The work opened up organizational issues that were thought to be untouchable. Through the social dreaming matrix, they found a way to free themselves of what were perceived as historical organizational constraints. A week after the seminar, the head nurse sent an inner-office memo round the hospital with the dreams that made an impact on her. It still hangs on the wall of her office.

He adds an ironic paragraph:

This is "ruining" my work! All everybody wants are dreams! Sometimes I feel that in the age of packaged seminars and the industry of awareness that has arisen in this millennium, people want a "quickie" with their social unconscious. I try very hard to hold on to the integrity of the dream.

Mike Teplitz <mteplitz@netvision.net.il>

One example from a company (out of many)

Italy: small company; presenting problem: improving communication and addressing the issue of cohesion. Franca Fubini (2003), an organizational consultant, decided to run a social dreaming matrix and to hold discussion groups. Time was of the essence in this project. The reality was that the company was being reorganized, and a third of the staff had been given notice of dismissal. In effect, the initial work was also a process of selecting those who were going to stay.

The first SDM was for the staff only, with no managers present. Having arranged the chairs in a snowflake pattern so that interaction between participants was limited, the task was stated as being to associate to the dreams presented to the matrix and to make links and find connections between the dreams. They followed the guidelines set out throughout this monograph.

After initial ironic comments along the lines of "they give us the sack and then give us a psychoanalyst to sweeten the pill", the participants settled down to the work of the matrix. The dreams expressed the anxiety that all were feeling in the company. There were *missed examinations, failed examinations, invalidated university degrees, shut doors, missed trains* reported in the dreams. As a result, they were able to associate to their anxieties at work with the uncertainty of their future.

In the next matrix the participants associated extensively and worked through the images it evoked of a dream. They were able to talk about the unrealistic expectations they had of their young firm existing as it did in a competitive environment.

The third matrix was for both staff and managers, who joined the original participants. The managers felt some anxiety, whereas the staff were full of glee. But soon they were on common ground as the dreams and associations flowed. The theme of *funerals* became dominant, allowing the participants to talk about the company's situation. Different options were aired for collaboration.

In the third, and final, matrix they reported that the matrix had acted as releasing the logjams that had been damming their progress. In some of the dreams there was the figure of *an old man who was loved or hated, dying or dead*. At a subsequent meeting with the founding members of the company, they referred to an older member who owned 32% of the shares. He did not work in the company but determined much of the policy because he had many political contacts in the outside environment.

Weeks later, when the consultant came for the final meeting, she was told that the partners had bought out the shares of "Mr 32%".

They had realized that the changes initiated were related primarily to

1. their own internal reorganization—they had reduced staff rather than looking at the need to update management;
2. a realistic evaluation of the changing market—they could

now see that the internal environment had to be in tune with the external one.

The material shows that pressures from the environment were leading to a collapse of the taken-for-granted establishment, and as a result a more realistic evaluation was demanded, and not one based on their desire for security and stability.

This example is mirrored in numerous others contained in *Social Dreaming @ Work* (Lawrence, 1998b) and *Experiences in Social Dreaming* (Lawrence, 2003), and also in journal articles, which are listed on the website for social dreaming:

www.socialdreaming.org

Social dreaming programmes are being hosted in churches in the United States. It has been discovered that the insights gained have informed practice in education, worship, and congregational life. In Germany, social dreaming is used in a university (Bergische) as part of a programme for training action researchers, with Inscape (contact: <inscape.coesfeld@ online.de>), and it has been used with the Austrian Social Democratic Party.

Social dreaming matrices have been organized for other specific groups of people—for example, Italian fire-fighters (<socialdreaming2004@yahoo.it>), and Italian students at La Sapienza University in Rome and at L'Aquila University. The social dreaming matrix is a feature of the Senior Management Programme of the King's Fund, London. Creative writers attending the Hay-on-Wye festival organized by the *Guardian* newspaper, have also benefited. In Bristol there are programmes of social dreaming (for details, see www.bristol. ac.uk/depts/conferences/rc/burwalls.html). In Spain, through IEEP (Instituto Europea de Estudios de Psicoterapia Psicoanalitica), Social Dreaming is run on a monthly basis by Julian Manley and Manuel Seijo.

Finally, since 1995 social dreaming has been part of the Programme for International Association for Analytical Psychology. Helen Morgan and Peter Tatham have held matrices in Zurich, Florence, and Cambridge, including one with 100 participants in this conference for Jungians.

REFERENCES AND FURTHER READING

Beradt, C. (1968). *The Third Reich of Dreams*. Chicago, IL: Quadrangle Books.

Bion, W. R. (1963). *Elements of Psycho-Analysis*. London: Karnac.

Bion, W. R. (1994). *Clinical Seminars and Other Works*. London: Karnac.

Bollas, C. (1987). *The Shadow of the Object*. London: Free Association Books.

Bollas, C. (1991). *Forces of Destiny*. London: Free Association Books.

Bollas, C. (2002). *Free Association*. Cambridge: Icon Books.

Capra, F. (1997). *The Web of Life*. London: Flamingo, Harper-Collins.

Capra, F. (2002). *The Hidden Connections*. London: Flamingo, Harper-Collins.

Christos, G. (2003). *Memory and Dreams*. New York: University of Rutgers Press.

Crick, F., & Mitchison, G. (1983). The function of dream sleep. *Nature, 304* (5922, July 14): 111–114.

De Duve, C. (1995). *Vital Dust*. New York: Basic Books, Harper-Collins.

Ehrenzweig, A. (1964). The undifferentiated matrix of artistic imagination. *Psychoanalytic Study of Society*, 3: 373–398.

Ehrenzweig, A. (1967). *The Hidden Order of Art: A Study in the Psychology of Artistic Imagination*. London: Weidenfeld &Nicholson. (Cited in: J. Gray, *Straw Dogs*. London: Granta Books, 2002.)

Erlich-Ginor, M. (2003). Sliding houses in the promised land. In: W. G. Lawrence, *Experiences in Social Dreaming* (pp. 157–178). London: Karnac, 2003.

Freud, S. (1900a). *The Interpretation of Dreams. S.E.*, 4.

Fubini, F. (2003). Social dreaming: Dreams in search of a dreamer. In: W. G. Lawrence, *Experiences in Social Dreaming* (pp. 259–266). London: Karnac Books.

Gray, J. (2002). *Straw Dogs*. London: Granta Books.

Greenstein, G. (1988). *The Symbiotic Universe*. New York: William Morrow.

Hartmann, E. (2000). The psychology and physiology of dreaming: A new synthesis. In: L. Gamwell (Ed.), *Dreams 1900–2000: Science, Art, and the Unconscious Mind*. New York: Cornell University Press.

James, C. (1994). "Social Dreaming and Living in the World." Unpublished manuscript.

Keve, T. (2000). *Triad: the Physicists, the Analysts, the Kabbalists*. London: Rosenberger & Krausz.

Keve, T. (2004). "Physics, Metaphysics and Psychoanalysts." Paper given at Conference: "Hungarian Psychoanalytic Ideas Revisited". Freud Museum and MLPC, London.

Lawrence, W. G. (1991). Won from the void and formless infinite: Experiences of social dreaming. *Free Associations*, 2 (Part 2, No. 22): 254–266.

Lawrence, W. G. (1994). The politics of salvation and revelation in the practice of consultancy. In: R. Casemore, G. Dyos, A. Eden, K. Kellner, J. McAuley, & S. Moss (Eds.), *What Makes Consultancy Work*. London: South Bank University Press.

Lawrence, W. G. (1998a). Social dreaming as a tool of action-research. In *Social Dreaming @ Work*. London: Karnac.

Lawrence, W. G. (1998b). *Social Dreaming @ Work*. London: Karnac.

Lawrence, W. G. (1999). The management of self in role. In: *Exploring Individual and Organizational Boundaries*. London: Karnac. [Originally published by John Wiley & Sons, Chichester. In German as: Selbtsmanagement-in-rollen. *Freie Assoziation, 1* (1/2).]

Lawrence, W. G. (2000a). Social dreaming illuminating social change. *Organisational & Social Dynamics, 1* (1): 78–93.

Lawrence, W. G. (2000b). *Tongued With Fire*. London: Karnac.

Lawrence, W. G. (2003) *Experiences in Social Dreaming*. London: Karnac.

Lawrence, W. G., & Biran, H. (2002). The complementarity of social dreaming and therapeutic dreaming. In: C. Neri, M. Pines, & R. Friedman (Eds.), *Dreams in Group Psychotherapy*. London: Jessica Kingsley.

Lifton, R. J. (1987). *The Future of Immortality*. New York: Basic Books.

Matte-Blanco, I. (1975). *The Unconscious as Infinite Sets*. London: Duckworth.

Matte-Blanco, I. (1988). *Thinking, Feeling, and Being*. London: Routledge.

Negroponte, N. (1995). *Being Digital*. London: Hodder & Stoughton.

Plato (c. 360 BC). *Timaeus*. Harmondsworth: Penguin, 1965.

Schachtel, E. G. (2001). On memory and childhood amnesia. In: *Metamorphosis* (pp. 279–322). Hillsdale, NJ: Analytic Press.

Stevenson, R. L. (1886). *The Strange Case of Dr Jekyll and Mr Hyde*. New York: Scribner.

Symington, J., & Symington, N. (1996). *The Clinical Thinking of Wilfred Bion*. London: Routledge.

Ullman, M. (1975). The transformation process in dreams. *American Academy of Psychoanalysis, 19* (2): 8–10.

Unamuno, M. de (1954). *The Tragic Sense of Life*. New York: Dover.

Wolf, F. A. (1994). *The Dreaming Universe*. New York: Simon & Schuster (Touchstone, 1995).

INDEX